Schoenberg: *Pierrot lunaire*

CAMBRIDGE MUSIC HANDBOOKS

GENERAL EDITOR Julian Rushton

Cambridge Music Handbooks provide accessible introductions to major musical works, written by the most informed commentators in the field.

With the concert-goer, performer and student in mind, the books present essential information on the historical and musical context, the composition, and the performance and reception history of each work, or group of works, as well as critical discussion of the music.

Other published titles

Bach: Mass in B Minor   JOHN BUTT
Beethoven: *Missa solemnis*   WILLIAM DRABKIN
Berg: Violin Concerto   ANTHONY POPLE
Handel: *Messiah*   DONALD BURROWS
Haydn: *The Creation*   NICHOLAS TEMPERLEY
Haydn: String Quartets, Op. 50   W. DEAN SUTCLIFFE
Janáček: *Glagolitic Mass*   PAUL WINGFIELD
Mahler: Symphony No. 3   PETER FRANKLIN
Musorgsky: *Pictures at an Exhibition*   MICHAEL RUSS
Schubert: *Die schöne Müllerin*   SUSAN YOUENS

Schoenberg: *Pierrot lunaire*

Jonathan Dunsby

Professor of Music
University of Reading

CAMBRIDGE
UNIVERSITY PRESS

Published by the Press Syndicate of the University of Cambridge
The Pitt Buildings, Trumpington Street, Cambridge CB2 1RP
40 West 20th Street, New York, NY 10011-4211, USA
10 Stamford Road, Oakleigh, Victoria 3166, Australia

First Published 1992

Printed in Great Britain at the University Press, Cambridge

A catalogue record for this book is available from the British Library

Library of Congress cataloguing in publication data
Dunsby, Jonathan.
Schoenberg. *Pierrot lunaire*/Jonathan Dunsby
p.   cm. – (Cambridge music handbooks)
Includes bibliographical references and index.
ISBN 0 521 38279 3 (hardback) – ISBN 0 521 38715 9 (paperback)
1. Schoenberg, Arnold, 1874–1951. *Pierrot lunaire*.
I. Title. II. Series.
ML410.S283D83   1992
782.4'7–dc20   91-36068   CIP   MN

ISBN 0521 38279 3 hardback
ISBN 0 521 38715 9 paperback

for Holly and Lulu

Contents

Preface

A few words about the intention and organization of what follows may help the reader. The first two chapters attempt to set the scene for *Pierrot lunaire* by describing the *commedia dell'arte* fashion of the early days of modernism, and by discussing Schoenberg's compositional career up to 1912. The later Schoenberg is not considered in this book except in passing. A brief third chapter outlines the genesis of Op. 21: this matter could itself be the topic of a monograph, and anyone who cares to follow up the specialized literature will discover a fascinating compositional story, on which I elaborate in the next and most substantial chapter. Chapter 4 goes through the twenty-one melodramas of *Pierrot* piece by piece, hoping to build a picture of the work overall – to offer a particular narrative path through it. Of course, there is not the remotest claim to say everything that might be said. I merely intended to say nothing that shouldn't be said. For better or worse I have avoided the presentation of technical analysis altogether, in the belief that there is need of a modern and accessible introduction to *Pierrot lunaire* for the reader to whom ramified theory is a long series of inevitably closed books; if I have stated the indefensible, I have failed accordingly. Chapter 5, an afterword, focuses on how *Pierrot* has been received in the twentieth century, substituting very few words for the many that could be written, have been, and I hope will be.

Acknowledgements

At the time of writing, Reinhold Brinkmann's edition of *Pierrot* for the Schoenberg Collected Edition has not been published. Professor Brinkmann has published significant findings along the way, on which I have relied and for which I record my gratitude.

I offer my personal thanks to: Penny Souster of Cambridge University Press for her confidence and calm tolerance; Julian Rushton, who backed me to the hilt without question, for his expert, painstaking advice on the drafts, all remaining inadequacies being my sole responsibility; and Alexander Goehr, who once upon a time – it is a long-standing debt – encouraged me both to study Schoenberg's music and to think about what it might really mean to be a composer. I am also grateful to Esther for her constant support.

Andrew Porter's permission to reproduce his translation of the text of *Pierrot lunaire* is gratefully acknowledged.

Reproduction of the music is acknowledged as follows:
Pierrot lunaire by Arnold Schoenberg
Poems by Albert Giraud
German text by Otto Erich Hartleben
Copyright © 1914 by Universal Edition
Copyright renewed 1941 by Arnold Schoenberg
Reproduced by permission of Alfred A. Kalmus Ltd.

The immortal Pierrot

Prologue

For all the rough critical ride Schoenberg's compositions have received in general, *Pierrot lunaire* has come to be regarded since its first performance in 1912 as a masterpiece. Wherever we look in the history of its reception, whether in general histories of the modern period, in more ephemeral press response, in the comments of musical leaders like Stravinsky or Boulez, in pedagogical sources, or in specialized research studies, the overwhelming reaction to *Pierrot* has been an awestruck veneration of its originality. No composition of the period seems to combine so many unusual features to such powerful effect. Schoenberg's masterly organization of the twenty-one poems, his constantly perfect touch in the expression of words in music, the creation of a new world of sound through a small ensemble from which is milked a constellation of textures as impressive in its variety as it is in its novelty, and of course his synthesis of these and many more elements into an emotionally haunting and unforgettable music–theatrical experience – all this has been admired, considered, absorbed by successive generations.[1] *Pierrot* has thus become one of the most highly-prized totems of modernism in musical composition, taking its place alongside Stravinsky's *The Rite of Spring* as a work that crosses virtually all ideological boundaries and has won the kind of cultural approval accorded to the 'masterpieces' of earlier musical ages. Every music student knows, and nearly every programme note in the audience's hands will mention, that Stravinsky dubbed *Pierrot* the 'solar plexus' of twentieth-century music (though in fact Stravinsky's various comments on the work are tinged with an irony which goes epigrammatically to the heart of some of the perceptual problems which anyone studying *Pierrot* must eventually confront: see, for example, pp. 37, 45 and 55 below).

None of this paean is recorded for the sake of paying further tribute to Schoenberg, nor is there any intention of trying to simplify the complex history of an extraordinarily complex work of art. On the contrary, the purpose of clarifying the extremes, even ideals, of progressivism, radicality and modernism that have been ascribed so often to *Pierrot* is to establish the best starting point for an understanding of the historical context of Schoenberg's creative outburst of 1912. For *Pierrot* did not spring unexpectedly from or into a cultural vacuum. Nothing ever does; but it is part of the beguiling aura surrounding *Pierrot* always to tend towards that impression.

So sure was Schoenberg's touch in his incubus of a clown that it is as if the Pierrot into whom he breathed life has gone on to shape his own history, to frighten us into believing that he emerged from nowhere, has no ancestors, no attachments and, most provocatively, cannot die. He shares this menacing immortality with Stravinsky's Petrushka, who thumbs his eternal nose at the Charlatan, *post mortem*, in the last moments of that ballet (1911). Yet Petrushka is much more nearly human than Pierrot. As Stephen Walsh puts it in his recent major study of Stravinsky's music, 'in the end *Petrushka* maintains a double aspect. The figure of the puppet himself is above all a late nineteenth-century creation, the misfit of romantic artistic mythology, less sentimentalized, certainly, than the pierrots of *Pagliacci* or *The Yeoman of the Guard*, but perpetuating the same essential conflict between the inward and the outward life.'[2] Schoenberg's Pierrot offers hardly any such consolations, regardless of whether we can fully accept the composer's avowed conception of creating a light, ironic and satirical tone.[3] Convinced he's been beheaded (No. 13), Pierrot bores open Cassander's skull to smoke a bowl of tobacco in it (No. 16), and at the end with consummate detachment can 'gladly view the lovely world'! He is, in human terms, absolutely outrageous. It is hard to imagine an ancestry, and much more comforting to believe that he and the composition in which he is embodied emerged from nowhere. The transformation of a genre, the death of a cult, and our century's commitment to modernism have created this illusion.

The genre

Melodrama – spoken words with musical accompaniment or musical interludes – was very much in vogue in the final years of the nineteenth century. History has proved it to be a passing fashion, albeit one that threw up an abiding masterpiece. That said, it was a significant and tenacious fashion, a burning issue of the day, the vitality of which it is hard for us now to recapture – as a result of which, as happens often and inevitably in the progress of musical historiography, neglect sets in. This is doubtless due in part to our view of the Classical period in which it had its ancestry being settled on the works of a handful of composers, Mozart towering at the top, so that more humdrum trends of that period receive scant attention. Among those trends was a taste for the combination of the spoken, that is declaimed, word, and music – and it is of course no accident that an anticipation of late-Romantic, pre-expressionist melodrama is to be found in the relatively wild emotionalism of eighteenth-century theatrical experiments. The earliest conspicuous 'melodrama' is usually held to be J.J. Rousseau's *Pygmalion* (1762) in which an actor's monologue alternates with music designed to express and enhance the sentiments of the drama. The idea was taken up by Georg Benda in *Ariadne* (1775), which is called a 'duo-drama with musical interludes', and many composers of the period followed the lead. In a well-known letter to his father from Mannheim, on 12 November 1778, Mozart conveys the excitement of this new genre:

The Seyler company are here, whom you no doubt already know by reputation; Herr von Dalberg is their manager. He refuses to let me go until I have composed a duodrama for him; and indeed it did not take me long to make up my mind, for I have always wanted to write a drama of this kind. I cannot remember whether I told you anything about this type of drama the first time I was here? On that occasion I saw a piece of this kind performed twice and was absolutely delighted. Indeed, nothing has ever surprised me so much, for I had always imagined that such a piece would be quite ineffective! You know, of course, that there is no singing in it, only recitation, to which the music is like a sort of obbligato accompaniment to a recitative. Now and then words are spoken while the music goes on, and this produces the finest effect.[4]

We know from a further letter of 3 December that Mozart was hard at work on a duodrama called *Semiramis*, which is now unfortunately completely lost.

Despite its auspicious beginnings, melodrama became a resource, a dramatic technique, rather than a genre. It was a highly visible one: German musicians and probably most others of the Romantic age knew the grave-digging scene in Beethoven's *Fidelio* and the incantation in Weber's *Freischütz*, for example; but it remained a special effect, not part of the expressive mainstream of the period. The failure of melodrama to thrive in the nineteenth century is most often put down to the success of other genres, indeed of other ways to compose music. For instance, what was perceived by Schumann, Brahms or Wolf as an exquisite model, in Schubert, of the Lied as a fusion of sung words and music, made it hardly likely that they would give serious attention to the interaction of spoken word and music (though Schumann did experiment in *Manfred*). As for the summits of musico-dramatic expression in the theatre, the high ground came to be occupied both in Verdi and Wagner by an ideal fusion in opera and music drama that is, to put it crudely, essentially musical. In Wagner this is true at least in the sense that the speech-song of the mature music dramas required a special kind of text, a stylized vocabulary and (in principle if not always in practice) rhyme scheme. This is quite the opposite aesthetic to the one, in the next generation, of *Pierrot*, which was going to be widely praised as the proof that music could be placed thoroughly at the service of a text, forming the 'parallelism on a higher level' to which Schoenberg himself referred.[5] Indeed in *Oper und Drama* Wagner explicitly rejected melodrama from his aesthetic. In one way and another then, excluded by the strongest musical impulses of the times, melodrama remained a quiescent genre for about a century. If its history does not detain us here, the justification is that this history did not detain Schoenberg either. His sources were much more immediate.

Different scholars attach different genealogies to the restitution of melodrama that took place in Europe at the end of the nineteenth century.[6] Most point to Richard Strauss's *Enoch Arden* (1897) as a symbol of the flowering of musical recitation; and it can be argued that the first version of Humperdinck's *Die Königskinder* (1897) deserves recognition for its actual notation of precise rhythms but approximate intervals, with which Schoenberg experimented in parts of the song-cycle *Gurrelieder*, on which he worked in 1900 and 1901. Tentatively, both the light and the serious in music were beginning to embrace the weapons of the theatre: in the sentimentality and innocent fun of operetta, and in the satirical, rebellious aura of the cabaret.

Cabaret was a prime breeding ground for new means of expression. It was within the conventions of cabaret that the conventions of a *fin-de-siècle* society could be ruthlessly challenged. The publication in 1900 of a volume of *Deutsche Chansons* compiled by Otto Bierbaum opened the floodgates of parody and satire. Schoenberg himself moved within this orbit in the early 1900s in Berlin, which was a main centre of European political disaffection, accepting an appointment as Musical Director of the *Überbrettl* in December 1901. He soon gave up this night-club work of making arrangements and writing songs, but he certainly entered into the spirit of the times: of his cabaret songs which have survived, at least one is not only musically charming but sets a positively, if satirically, obscene text – this from the man who in later life was to be seen as, and surely was, a guardian of the highest spiritual values in art as in life. It is possible that Schoenberg turned away from the *Überbrettl* circle because of what has come to be regarded as its inherent decadence, a decadence which was pervasive in the tormented turmoil of central Europe before the First World War. It is hardly to be doubted, though, that his experience of the merciless, pristine, razor-sharp forms of expression of the Berlin night-club world was an important ingredient in the comprehensive skills which he would bring to *Pierrot*, the world in which one of the central ideologues was Otto Erich Hartleben, who was, to all intents and purposes, the librettist of Op. 21.[7]

Just as important as the historical swirls and eddies – and not, as we are in the course of discovering, a vacuum – from which *Pierrot* arose, is a sense of the quite irresistible cultural forces which were driving Western art into unknown spheres of experience, into 'modernism'. Wassily Kandinsky put this with outstanding conviction at the beginning of his essay 'On the question of form' in *Der 'Blaue Reiter' Almanac*, an artistic manifesto of 1912 in which leading expressionist artists offered their wares and ideas, not least Schoenberg, who contributed an essay, and the song *Herzgewächse* which will be discussed in due course: 'At a certain time', wrote Kandinsky,

what is inevitable ripens, i.e., the creative *spirit* (which could be called the abstract spirit) makes contact with the soul, later with other souls, and awakens a yearning, an inner urge.

When the conditions necessary for the maturation of a certain form are met, the yearning, the inner urge, the force is strengthened so that it can create a new value in the human spirit that consciously or unconsciously begins to live in man.

Consciously or unconsciously man tries, from this moment on, to find a material form for the spiritual form, for the new value that lives within him.[8]

Schoenberg was, at the very time these ideas were penned (1911), yearning to create something like *Pierrot*, and found in the newly revived genre of melodrama one crucial aspect of the 'material form' he needed: he might well have used Mozart's very words, 'I have always wanted to compose this type of drama'.

To prevent confusion over the term 'genre', the obvious needs to be stated – that the supporting generic type of Op. 21 is the song-cycle. When we consider the way that Schoenberg organized his plot in choosing and ordering certain poems from a larger collection, it is clear that one of his compositional means of maintaining order, in the bizarre new expressionist world in which he began to sketch early in 1912, was the tradition of the song-cycle, and, purely musically, the tradition of the integrated collection, or 'multi-piece' as it has been termed. (Pierrot and his commedia companions had already figured in this tradition, each assigned their piece in Schumann's 'Scènes mignonnes sur quatre notes', that is, *Carnaval*, of 1834–5.)

Although *Pierrot* has dominated many of the musical trends of the present century, it did not, after all, lead to a sustained new genre of melodrama. Modern music has cast its net so wide in means and manner that the mere interaction of speech and music is a tame resource, and even the heightened speech/subordinated song of Schoenberg's *Sprechstimme*, with its hint of fixed pitch and continual glissandi (akin to Messiaen's *Ondes Martenot*), could not become a lasting model. Works as diverse as Stravinsky's *Perséphone* (1934) and Walton's *Façade* (1923), indeed Schoenberg's own *Ode to Napoleon* of 1942, all use declamation with music, but in a distinctly conservative manner. With our hindsight, it is certainly reasonable to argue, as Peter Branscombe does in his *New Grove Dictionary* article on 'Melodrama', that 'the use of music as an adjunct to dramatic action is probably almost as old as drama itself', and that there can be little case for regarding melodrama as a distinct dramatic genre.[9] Yet the fashion for melodrama, and for a much less constrained attitude towards the interaction of music and text, saw the birth of a new kind of expression. Schoenberg's *Sprechstimme* led the path to subsequent widespread investigations of new types of vocal sound, pitched, unpitched, 'extended' in hitherto unimagined ways, more recently through the use of sound amplification which greatly expands the compositional possibilities. Thus *Pierrot* has transcended what from our perspective may be called the conventional, if excitingly new, generic garb in which he first appeared; hence his magical illusion in stimulating a perpetual modernism.

The commedia cult

Gradually, half the artists of Europe, and the United States, fell under the fascination of the commedia in the period from 1890 to 1930. The process began in Paris, spread to Munich and St Petersburg and later to London and New York. We say 'spread' partly to mean the way this message was communicated from city to city, but partly to suggest the variety of forms taken by this cult of the commedia.[10]

The litany of creative minds who rekindled images of the centuries-old *commedia dell'arte* figures is long and impressive. It centres to some extent around Diaghilev and the commedia ballet, but Diaghilev alone could not have imposed the commedia cult so pervasively in all the arts, on Picasso,

T.S. Eliot, Nijinsky, Chaplin, Meyerhold, in a large *dramatis personae* for which the phrase 'half the artists of Europe, and the United States' is perfectly reasonable. In music, the range of composers who contributed to the cult is astonishing to anyone who happens not to have noticed it, covering the continent by longitude and latitude (Busoni, Debussy, Puccini; de Falla, Walton, Bartók). Any list of the music at issue is, admittedly, likely to be as long as the definition of commedia is broad. The commedia figures distilled by the cult – moonstruck Pierrot, his idol the feckless Columbine, who degrades herself by giving in to the brutal Harlequin, who closes the vicious circle by his mocking camaraderie with Pierrot – these are themselves somewhat gruesome representations of that Western archetype, the eternal triangle.

It can hardly be claimed that any opera libretto in which two men vie in the conquest of one woman is part of the cult. However, at the turn of the century many composers began to make deliberate use of fundamental characteristics of the commedia characters: often their actual names; their disembodiment, usually as marionettes or puppets; and their lack of rootedness which symbolized the cruel alienation of the times - which Pierrot has a mother? which Harlequin a cherished cousin? The traditional screaming baby of the British Punch and Judy theatre is a softened image compared with the harsh European commedia cult, which was often tinged with a symbolic challenge to heterosexual hegemony, and perceived at the time as a most threatening homosexual haemorrhage. Similarly, commedia characters are themselves individual representations of central human caricatures, such as the zany foolish clown (*zanni* – originally – in Italian street theatre of the sixteenth century). Whereas Leoncavallo's *I Pagliacci* (1892) can well be drawn into the canon of cult works, the mere stardom of foolishness is no guarantee – perhaps the most famous pure foolery of all, that of Wagner's Parsifal, 'der reine Tor', on his hunt for the grail (1877–82), inhabits an entirely distinct cultural milieu.

If the need for fine distinctions is accepted, it is nevertheless incontestable that the scent of commedia was strong in the air of symbolist and expressionist art and literature. Louisa Jones conveys this excellently in her lively account of literature and the popular comic arts of nineteenth-century France: 'beginning with the magic carnivals of Rimbaud, the sacred clowns of Mallarmé, the mystic tricksters of Apollinaire[,the] nineteenth century created a wardrobe of masks and poses, a repertory of patterns and associations – many of them clichés – which individual writers and painters [and musicians] later drew on at will'.[11] And that repertory was well used. As Susan Youens points out in an article about the allegorical nature of the text of *Pierrot lunaire*, 'Pierrots were endemic everywhere in late nineteenth-/early twentieth-century Europe as an archetype of the self-dramatizing artist, whose stylized mask both symbolizes and veils artistic ferment.'[12] This comment is interesting because of its implicit suggestion of a link between past and future at the turn of the century. The 'self-dramatizing artist' is, after all, a concept we are more likely to associate with nineteenth-century Romanticism than subsequent modernism.

The pervasiveness of the commedia cult is stressed here because in at least two areas of the received view of early twentieth-century music there has been, as it were, a kink in the unrolling of historiography. On the one hand, writers on music of the period have on the whole concentrated on describing the crisis in musical 'language' that emerged with the spread of so-called 'atonality' (a significant and fairly recent case in point is Jim Samson's book *Music in Transition*). The social and, indeed, artistic context of musical composition of the period has received less attention, perhaps naturally enough, but as a result the conceptual characteristics of music of this period have often escaped notice. I have discussed in the article '*Pierrot lunaire* and the resistance to theory' what great care is needed when interpreting early critiques of *Pierrot*. They often conceal, under the guise of specific criticism, an attitude to the composer, and indeed to the radicalism of art in general before the First World War, rather than to the work.

On the other hand, and more particularly, since every sympathetic writer on Schoenberg's *Pierrot* is obliged to praise its many kinds of radicalism, we can easily lose sight of the obvious, that Schoenberg was bound to write a commedia work at some point. Only an imperious historical hindsight could claim that it was inevitable. But it should hardly surprise us, though Schoenberg historians have tended to let the originality, freshness, surprise of the composer's Op. 21 as a whole seep into its more or less predictable commedia aspect. The time was just right. Perhaps this is what Webern meant when he wrote to Berg about Schoenberg's new commission, commenting that the maestro had 'had something of the sort in mind for a long time'.[13]

This leads us back to the idea outlined above of how Schoenberg's Pierrot made himself immortal, not only through the transformation of a genre (the melodrama), but also the death of a cult. Historians seem to be in general agreement that, if it can be argued that a commedia cult held sway from about 1890, it must also be argued that it disappeared during the 1930s. The very conspicuousness of its occasional reappearance, for instance in Harrison Birtwistle's opera *Punch and Judy* (1967), is testimony that other conceptual characteristics have taken the stage in recent decades. This is in no small measure a result of Pierre Boulez's *Le Marteau sans maître* (1953–55), in which there was presented an exciting and influential change of focus in the 'parallelism on a higher level' which Schoenberg had announced in *Der 'Blaue Reiter'* in 1912. 'In *Pierrot lunaire'*, according to Boulez, 'the vocalist *narrates* and her role is to *speak* and to *act* a text. In *Le Marteau sans maître* she *sings* a poetic proposition, which sometimes occupies the forefront of the picture and is sometimes absorbed into the musical context.'[14] Narration and acting, ambiguities of perceived style and aesthetic, the knowing nod – these are the foundations of commedia, which could not hope to survive in Boulez's new environment of a style 'free of any oblique references'.

The cult is long gone, but *Pierrot* has outlived it. Its qualities of greatness lay not in its fashionable elements, though it represented those too – even though music history as a whole has chosen to ignore them. They lay in its ability to recreate the world of sensibility from which it emerged. If the modern audience attending *Pierrot* perceives not a world of sensibility but an occasion when a particular sensibility is conjured up and believed in at the time, no harm is done. An audience is not a historical conference.

Modernism

Now in the last decades of the twentieth century, we have reached a point when we can begin to see the effects of time at work in music composed earlier in the century. Some composers who were well known in their own era are now forgotten; others endure by repeated performances of their work. Musicians today continue to study and perform, for example, the music of Arnold Schoenberg. There is a mastery and substance to it that goes deeper than a thorny surface that continues to baffle many listeners. Schoenberg's music has nonetheless endured, and it now makes a living and lasting contribution to our culture.[15]

With the genre and the cult gone, the 'thorny surface' of *Pierrot* remains, and, though 'baffle' is a strong term, threaded throughout this volume will be found indications of how inherently ungraspable *Pierrot* is. It may be argued, quite reasonably, that most of the art of modern Western Europe is ungraspable in various senses anyway. For instance, our own experiences as human beings lead to continual development: what we hear in a piece one year will not be what we hear in it the next. Memory too decays and leads to expectations, on re-hearing familiar music, that are challenged by the unexpected, for we will always have retained a less than perfect image of the work of art (this creditable notion is expounded by Leonard Meyer in *Emotion and Meaning in Music*). Modes of performance alter the musical 'object', sometimes almost beyond the boundaries of kinship, if not identity – a *Pierrot* sung by a woman who always tries to hit the exact pitch at least at the beginning of each note is hardly the same work in experience (though it so firmly is in common-sense reality) as a *Pierrot* in which the *Sprechstimme* swoops and glides with no hard reference to the notated points of absolute pitch (which is, technically, a lot easier to do if the singer does not have 'perfect pitch').

Western art is a mobile, fluid experience for any one observer. If it were not, a few seconds looking at a masterly painting would do for life, and nothing would be gained from attending *Don Giovanni* more than once. The concert-goer must be presumed to hold to this view of the mobility and fluidity of perception, for if not the 'stock' repertoire would become unbearably boring, and the audience would constantly seek out new music. Yet against that has to be set a fundamental, or at least long-term, pessimism, of the kind summarized by Arnold Whittall:

the common conclusion is that the modern age, with its unprecedented social and national conflicts and its remarkable technological and intellectual advances, is simply not an age in which worthwhile art can be expected to flourish: it is too unstable, too diffused, and art reflects this without being able to transcend it - hence, in music, the emphasis on discord, fragmentation and sheer diversity of style.[16]

Schoenberg himself, though, did not believe that 'discord, fragmentation and sheer diversity of style' posed an inevitable threat even to the greatest art, let alone the merely 'worthwhile'. He felt that his music would become as overestimated in the future as it had been underestimated in the past. This was not the wishful thinking of an immodest mind, but a statement of faith in his work together with a frank recognition that worthwhile art inevitably tends to suppress that which is only marginally less worthwhile: he knew that Brahms's legacy had virtually destroyed Raff's, and the Haydn–Mozart–Beethoven estate had eliminated virtually every good Classical composer from subsequent attention (nor, obviously, is this inevitable mechanism restricted to musical culture).

It is precisely the diffusion of twentieth-century art that testifies to the quality of what has endured. Schoenberg's whole *œuvre* was a major factor in the creation of that modernism which sustains it. His movement from tonal consolidation, through the 'crisis' of atonality, to a permutational approach (in the dodecaphonic works) represents, at least as far as the disposition of musical pitch is concerned, the fragmentation of modernism. Each subsequent composer reacts to the elements with different emphasis, but overall few are willing to choose finally in that 'living and lasting contribution' (see note 15) between, say, *Verklärte Nacht* (1899), *Pierrot* (1912) and the Fourth String Quartet (1936).

If this more optimistic picture of the twentieth century has some weight, it must be of significance in explaining how *Pierrot*, so superficially anchored in its time and even place, survives. There is among musicians worldwide, beleaguered and otherwise, a core of commitment to the sort of modernism Schoenberg created, far from single-handedly, but centrally; a refusal to release certain repertoire for ever into the abyss of rejected styles; a fascination and enlightenment in trying to grasp the ungraspable. And thus, to return to the perhaps fanciful anthropomorphism indulged in twice already in this account, Pierrot in 1912 was creating his own immortality, marking out for good his disturbingly alien place.

Schoenberg 1908–1912

Schoenberg composed *Pierrot* when he was thirty-seven years old. It was his twenty-first opus, and that there were twenty-one melodramas was more than a happy coincidence. He was fascinated by numerology, magic, the supernatural, any aspect of the world of the spirit. Age did not diminish his superstitions: to the end he maintained his well-practised solution to what, of a more lowly mind, would be called a neurosis about the numbering of bars, '11, 12, 12a, 14, 15'. In his mid-thirties, he had undergone a formidable personal crisis which can only have reinforced his instinct to fear the worst, and fight it. The year, 1908, has come to be seen as a turning point in the history of music (by this time he had already completed a symphonic poem and a chamber symphony, two sets of orchestral songs and four sets for voice and piano, two quartets – one of which was published only posthumously – and one string sextet). Only the basic facts have ever emerged; if there is a record of some of the thoughts, feelings, heights and horrors involved, it remains hidden. The expressionist painter Richard Gerstl, nine years Schoenberg's junior, gave painting lessons to both the composer and his wife Mathilde, and lived in the same block. Mathilde left Schoenberg to live with Gerstl. When she moved back, Gerstl committed suicide.

Why, in delving into Schoenberg's musical development, is this tragic story recounted without fail, usually embroidered with as many details as each author can deem plausible? It is just an assumption – that matters of life, death and love can be traced in and must somehow inform a person's creative work. Thus, for Malcolm MacDonald, 'the events of 1908 provoked in Schoenberg an emotional and creative upsurge of daunting intensity',[1] and the Second String Quartet written at this time echoed, according to Adorno, 'a crisis in personal life whose sorrow, hardly ever mastered, brought to Schoenberg's work its full creative weight'.[2] Perhaps so. Perhaps Schoenberg continued to paint, as well as compose, until he had worked away his feelings about the morbid Gerstl affair. Perhaps this is what his son-in-law Felix Greissle meant many years later by commenting that 'Schoenberg was not a painter. He painted for entirely different reasons. It's a very private matter. And when this didn't exist anymore, he didn't paint anymore'.[3] And perhaps – who could resist the thought? – Pierrot is the composer, and part of the purity of vision in *Pierrot* is that Columbine and Harlequin are treated with such restraint by Schoenberg's choice of twenty-one poems from fifty that were available – Columbine yearned for just once and hopelessly in No. 2, Harlequin banished from the script. To follow the speculation mercilessly, perhaps after all there is not quite such dignity, if Cassander, trepanned, smoked in and played upon with a giant viola bow in Nos. 16 and 19, were Schoenberg's resurrection of Gerstl. The speculation is as endless as it is compulsive, but as Hildesheimer warns us in his influential psycho-biography of Mozart, the historian has a duty to be cautious, to avoid 'trite biographies: they find easy explanations for everything, within a range of probability we can comprehend. The primary source and the motivation are the same: wishful thinking'.[4]

However that may be, *Pierrot* stands nearly at the end of a spectacular surge in Schoenberg's work which began in 1907 and took wing in 1908. There are many easily available descriptions of the resulting repertoire. Willi Reich's critical biography (1971) is both compact and informative, as is Malcolm MacDonald's contribution on Schoenberg to the Master Musicians series (1976). Luigi Rognoni's *The Second Vienna School* (1977) sets 'atonal' period works not only in the context of Schoenberg's entire development, but that of his pupils Berg and Webern as well. Charles Rosen's *Schoenberg* (1976), short and simply written, is the outstanding account of what it is that makes this composer a 'modern master', and is particularly interesting about the atonal works. As will become evident in the present volume, there is much too to be learned from Schoenberg's own writings in *Style and Idea*, some 500 pages of essays, greatly expanding the original short collection which was published in 1950, the year before Schoenberg's death.

There has developed a tendency to cite the Second String Quartet, Op. 10, as Schoenberg's ground-breaking score, because of its use of the medium (the two final movements are for soprano and quartet), because the finale has no key signature, and because its premiere in December 1908 caused uproar in the auditorium and extreme rudeness in the press – comments that Schoenberg was 'tone deaf' and the like. Schoenberg puts more emphasis on *Das Buch der hängenden Gärten* (The Book of the Hanging Gardens), Fifteen Songs, Op. 15 (1908–9):

I was inspired by poems of Stefan George, the German poet, to compose music to some of his poems, and, surprisingly, without any expectation on my part, these songs showed a style quite different from everything I had written before. And this was only the first step on a new path, but one beset with thorns. It was the first step towards a style which has since been called the style of 'atonality'. Among progressive musicians it aroused great enthusiasm. New sounds were produced, a new kind of melody appeared, a new approach to expression of moods and characters was discovered. In fact, it called into existence a change of such an extent that many people, instead of realizing its evolutionary element, called it a revolution.[5]

The *George-Lieder*, favourite grist for the music theorists' mill, less so for the historians', were certainly progressive, in their virtual absence of major–minor tonality, and in their sparse economy of expression. These characteristics are to be found, however, in earlier compositions, if to a less radical degree. That is what Schoenberg means, in part, by the word 'evolutionary'. In this stage of his argument in what was originally a lecture delivered in 1937, from which the words above are quoted, and in which he was constrained by the medium to suppress many more insights than the few which could be presented, he chooses to put Op. 15 on the necessary pedestal. Curiously, after a discussion of Op. 10 which amounts to the idea that an audience of the time could not have been expected to understand the music after only one hearing, he proceeds to talk, with immense satisfaction, of the First Chamber Symphony, Op. 9, which he calls 'my next work'. Yet in fact Op. 9 was composed two years earlier than Op. 10, and premiered a year earlier; Schoenberg had a perfectly good memory in 1937, and was not a habitually careless thinker. Is this a residue of personal suffering? In later life, did mental confusion return when he had to recall the years around 1908? The title of the lecture, which recounts how from one short era to the next his audiences could not understand his progress, is most striking: 'How One Becomes Lonely'.

By 1949, at least, in an essay entitled 'My Evolution', the clear hindsight of a seventy-four-year-old is in evidence. 'The climax of my first period is definitely reached in the *Kammersymphonie*, Op. 9', he writes. Then:

My Two Ballads, Op. 12, were the immediate predecessors of the Second String Quartet, Op. 10, which marks the transition to my second period. In this period I renounced a tonal centre – a procedure incorrectly called 'atonality'. In the first and second movements there are many sections in which the individual parts proceed regardless of whether or not their meetings result in codified harmonies. Still, here, and also in the third and fourth movements, the key is presented distinctly at all the main dividing-points of the formal organization. Yet the overwhelming multitude of dissonances cannot be counterbalanced any longer by occasional returns to such tonal triads as represent a key. It seemed inadequate to force a movement into the Procrustean bed of tonality without supporting it by harmonic progressions that pertain to it. This dilemma was my concern, and it should have occupied the minds of all my contemporaries also. That I was the first to venture the decisive step will not be considered universally a merit – a fact I regret but have to ignore.

This first step occurred in the Two Songs, Op. 14, and thereafter in the *Fifteen Songs of the Hanging Gardens* [*sic*] and in the Three Piano Pieces, Op. 11.[6]

Once again Op. 15 appears centre-stage, but now in company, and it is in Op. 11 that the 'step' seems to take place within the course of the composition itself (as also in Op. 10). The three incipits shown in examples 1a–c indicate – albeit misrepresenting most of the music in the sense that each piece goes on to present rich, new material, with significant contrast in both Nos. 1 and 2 – this progress from a post-Brahms style, through a brooding but tonally suggestive 'slow movement', to the liberated expressionist atonality which Schoenberg regarded as such a momentous discovery, and which the rigours of twelve-note composition would eventually have to control: 'Intoxicated by the enthusiasm of having freed music from the shackles of tonality, I had thought to find further liberty of expression. In fact, I myself and my pupils Anton von Webern and Alban Berg, and even Alois Hába believe that now music could renounce motivic features and remain coherent and comprehensible nevertheless.'[7] The piano figured large in Schoenberg's output, and it was to figure again before *Pierrot* in the Six Little Piano Pieces, Op. 19 (1911), miniatures of such concentrated expression, and with no text to sustain invention, that they are over in a few minutes. In this sense they parallel the Five Orchestral Pieces, Op. 16, of 1909, in which 'formal expansion does not accompany the extension of expressive range: as Schoenberg later observed, brevity and intensity of expression are interdependent in these pieces'.[8] No. 6 of Op. 19 is probably Schoenberg's only finished composition of which it can be said that anyone who reads music is able to play the right notes at about the right time (performing it well is quite a different matter). Even this short but powerful set of pieces made Schoenberg nervous in respect of the particular public who had so hurtfully failed to warm to the genius in their midst, and whom he left to go to Berlin in the autumn of 1911. He wrote to Berg on 3 April 1912 from Berlin (this was the day after he had completed 'Der Dandy', No. 3 of *Pierrot* in the order on which he eventually settled): 'I am not allowing any new works to be performed in Vienna at the moment, as I

Ex. 1: Three Piano Pieces, Op. 11: opening bars of each piece

find that Vienna hurts me abroad. For that reason I want you to return my manuscript [Op. 19] to me as soon as possible.'⁹

Herzgewächse, Op. 20, a short song for soprano, celeste, harmonium and harp, has already been mentioned as part of the *Blaue Reiter* manifesto (see p. 5 above). It shows Schoenberg primed for continuing labour at forming new kinds of sound, as the instrumentation alone suggests. Over the years many of his own comments about *Pierrot* refer with most enthusiasm to its new sounds: 'But the prettiest story last: a short while back . . .[a] *lift-man* asked me whether it was I who had written *Pierrot lunaire*. For he had heard it before the war (about 1912), at the first performance, and still had the sound of it in his ears, particularly of one piece where red jewels were mentioned [No. 10, 'Raub'].'¹⁰ *Herzgewächse* also encapsulates the strenuous task performers were to have in atonal music and beyond. At bar 27 the soprano has to sing a long f''', far higher than the customary range (and nearly always mentioned whenever Op. 20 is mentioned). There were to be no compromises. Composers writing music at limits no one had before imagined would set previously unattainable limits for performers. The severity of the next challenge, the *Sprechstimme* in Op. 21, was a logical step, evolution rather than revolution.¹¹

Meanwhile Schoenberg had been pursuing a post-Wagnerian course in *Die glückliche Hand*, Op. 18, (literally, 'The Lucky Hand', or 'The Hand of Fate') on which he worked from 1910 to 1913. Even though this 'drama with music' is shorter than the next 'opera', it cost the composer a great deal of labour if only because of the many creative processes involved. He wrote his own text, about the creative hero whose female mate is lured away by other men, and designed his own lighting and staging, involving a chorus of twelve who intone (partly in a version of *Sprechstimme*) the moral of the tale – that the price of creative success is repeated, self-induced personal failure.

Finally, the scene is set for *Pierrot* by *Erwartung* ('Anticipation'), which Schoenberg called an opera – half an hour of music for soloist and orchestra, usually referred to as a monodrama, and which he claimed to have composed in fourteen days, August to September 1909. There is a special kinship between *Erwartung* and *Pierrot* in that neither has a conventional narrative. In *Pierrot*, although each poem has the same formal pattern including textual repetition which produces a sense of continuous organizational control, there is no real 'story' overall, but rather a succession of images, ideas, actions, moods: the mind of the listener races to find a narrative logic, like the logic we use to recall the dissociated images of a dream. Schoenberg said that *Erwartung* could be comprehended as a nightmare, and the narrative logic of the half-hour 'plot' offers little alternative – at night, a woman searches a forest for her lover, whom she quickly finds, murdered, then she recalls their feelings in a shattered subliminal logic. The text was written by a medical student, Marie Pappenheim, and reflects the topical first blush of the age of psychoanalysis: the following extract, from the end of *Erwartung*, provides a flavour of this:

Light will dawn for all others . . .
but I, all alone in my darkness?
Morning separates us . . . always morning . . .
How heavy your parting kiss . . .
Another interminable day of waiting . . .
but you won't wake up again.
A thousand people pass by . . .
I cannot pick you out.
All are alive, their eyes aflame . . .
Where are you?

It is dark . . .
your kiss, like a beacon in my darkness . . .
my lips burn and gleam . . . towards you . . .
Oh, you are here . . .
I was seeking . . .

One reason why *Erwartung* is so significant in the expressionist backdrop of *Pierrot* is that it proved the possibility of sustained musical representation of a totally new order: it proceeds not only without, as Rosen puts it so well, 'all the traditional means by which music was supposed to make itself intelligible: repetition of themes, integrity and discursive transformation of clearly recognizable motifs . . . harmonic structures based on a framework of tonality'; but also without a conventional textual narrative. It is not only the 'apparently total freedom from the requirements of musical form' that has made *Erwartung* 'a well-attested miracle, inexplicable and incontrovertible',[12] but also its freedom from traditional dramatic narrative.

Thus the scene was set:

I may tell you frankly that much as I liked the compositions I wrote at this time, I was equally afraid to have them submitted to the public . . . But then two of my new works caused a complete change in the situation: my *Harmonielehre* (Theory of Harmony), published in 1911, and *Pierrot lunaire*, a cycle of poems declaimed to the accompaniment of chamber orchestra. Until then, I had been considered only a destroyer, and even my craftsmanship had been doubted, in spite of the many works of my first period. The *Harmonielehre* endowed me with the respect of many former adversaries who hitherto had considered me a wild man, a savage, an illegitimate intruder into musical culture. These same people were forced now to realize that they were wrong . . . And so I approached rather rapidly the first climax when *Pierrot* gave me a great success by the novelty which it offered in so many respects.[13]

However briefly, this discussion has shown the main elements on which Schoenberg was able to draw in the spring of 1912. His fascination with symbolist poetry and theatre, and his own brilliant literary sensibility, had made him an experienced user of experimental narrative, whether his own or others'. In one work after another – chamber programme music, single-movement quartet, chamber symphony, quartet with singer – he had shown a special ability to escape generic constraints, to find new forms and new sounds. It had been established beyond doubt, or beyond the doubt of the composer, his pupils, his friends such as the painters Kokoschka and Kandinsky, the writer Karl Kraus, architect Adolph Loos, that traditional organizational means of music, above all tonality, but also thematic repetition and motivic development, were not essential to musical coherence. And, personally, he was a driven man at the first height of his creative powers, before the long period of reflection and re–evaluation which was to lead to the early twelve-note compositions.

3

Genesis

The composition of *Pierrot* has been quite fully documented. The first summation of the known estate of Schoenberg was in Josef Rufer's *The Works of Arnold Schoenberg* (1962, published originally in German in 1959). Rufer was able to draw attention to the manuscript of *Pierrot* in the Library of Congress, and to various other materials that indicate facts about the composition of the work. Rufer's work is now out of date. On *Pierrot*, it was superseded by Jan Maegaard's *Studien . . . (Studies in the Development of Dodecaphonic Composition in Arnold Schoenberg,* 1972), a work of detailed scholarship based on examination of all the materials that were to be housed from 1976 in the Archive of the Arnold Schoenberg Institute in Los Angeles, the city where Schoenberg settled in 1934. More recently, the editor of *Pierrot* for the Collected Edition of Schoenberg's music, Reinhold Brinkmann, published 'What the sources tell us: a chapter of *Pierrot* philology', an authoritative article about the genesis of the work.[1] Detailed musicological research can sometimes turn received opinion on its head, and this is no less true of Schoenberg than of other composers: for, instance, some of the early, 1930s, accounts of his 'twelve-tone system' were quite wrong. However, what the widely-consulted books say about the genesis and structure of *Pierrot* is largely true – the reader may well encounter, for example, William Austin's trustworthy *Music in the Twentieth Century* (1966), one of the few general musical histories of this period to discuss *Pierrot* in relative detail. The discussion in this chapter will be brief, since details about Schoenberg's working practices in 1912 are assimilated in chapter 4.

Albert Giraud's 1884 cycle of fifty poems, entitled *Pierrot lunaire*, was translated into German, and considerably improved, by Otto Erich Hartleben. From the 1911 edition of this work, Schoenberg studied and selected twenty-one poems, having been commissioned by Albertine Zehme to compose a cycle of melodramas.

Mrs Zehme, a former actress, had for some time been drawn to the commedia dell'arte character of Pierrot. Having discovered Giraud's cycle of poems, *Pierrot lunaire*, translated by E. O. Hartleben and composed as 'melodrama' by Vrieslander [these are in fact simply songs], Mrs Zehme toured Germany declaiming these piquant and somewhat bizarre lyrics. But the music was obviously not strong enough, and someone advised her to approach Schoenberg, who was also considered 'bizarre', to say the least, and at this time not very well known, for it was before the performance of *Gurrelieder*, an event which made him world famous.[2]

Schoenberg first heard of his commission on 25 January 1912, signed the contract for a voice and piano composition on 9 March, began to notate the work on 12 March, and essentially finished *Pierrot* in mid-July (and not September, as used to be thought). The composer had been in Berlin since the autumn of 1911, lecturing on aesthetics and composition at the Stern Conservatory, and was in a fallow, depressed period. He noted on 12 March: 'I had already thought about the possibility that I would never compose again at all'.

Surviving materials show that Schoenberg was certain about twenty of the twenty-one poems (No. 21, 'O alter Duft', the last melodrama to be begun, on 30 May, may have been an afterthought) and planned a cycle in approximately equal halves. The decision to offer 'Three times Seven Poems', numbers of mystical significance, made a cycle of twenty-one, which is the opus number of *Pierrot*, as he knew it would be. He began with what is now No. 9, 'Gebet an Pierrot', asking Zehme's leave to use a clarinet, and over a period of about four weeks had finally determined the instruments and personnel.

Table 1 charts Schoenberg's use of five players and their eight instruments.

There has been some misinformation, often taken up by the popular musical press over the decades, about the precise disposition of instrumental forces in *Pierrot*. Even Egon Wellesz, a close associate of Schoenberg who wrote the first book about his music, invites criticism by writing that 'every poem is differently orchestrated',[3] and commentary is sometimes simply wrong – for example, 'each piece is scored for voice and two or three of the instruments' in Gerald Abraham's *A Hundred Years of Music*.[4] Certainly, the same combination is not used twice in the same way. How Schoenberg lists the instruments in the Universal Edition score makes this clear: No. 14, for instance, is scheduled (translated here) for 'piano, and later flute, clarinet in A, violin, cello', but No. 15 is for 'clarinet in A, violin, piano, and later flute and cello'. Literally, at least it can be said, as in one of

Table 1

	Short title	Pf.	Fl.	Pic.	Cl.*	BCl.	Vn.	Va.	Vc.
						Instruments			
1	Mondestrunken	x	x				x		x
2	Colombine	x	x		x		x		
3	Dandy	x		x	x				
4	Wäscherin		x		x		x		
5	Valse	x	x		x	x			
6	Madonna	†	†			†	†		†
7	Mond		x						
8	Nacht	x				x			x
9	Gebet	x			x				
10	Raub		x		x		x		x
	[Transition]	x							
11	Messe	†		†		†		†	†
12	Galgenlied			x				x	x
13	Enthauptung	x				x		x	x
	[Transition]		x			x		x	x
14	Kreuze	†	†		†		†		†
15	Heimweh	x			x		x		
	[Transition]	†		†	†		†		†
16	Gemeinheit	†		†	†		†		†
17	Parodie	x		x	x			x	
	[Transition]	x							
18	Mondfleck	†		†	†		†		†
19	Serenade	x							†
	[Transition]	†	†		†		†		†
20	Heimfahrt	†	†		†		†		†
21	Duft	†	†	†	†	†	†	†	†

x = instrument is used
† = instrument is used and all five instrumentalists are playing
* = clarinet is in A except in 'Der Mondfleck', which calls for clarinet in B♭.

the most recently published histories of twentieth-century music, that 'each of the twenty-one pieces of the cycle *introduces* a different combination'.[5]

Even a raw count of the number of songs in which each instrument is used is confounded by Nos. 5 and 21 with their various doublings, and a better count might be by player (pianist 17 out of 21, flautist 16, clarinettist 19, violinist 15, cellist 13).[6] And even this statistic is of little interest to the cellist, who appears least often but has to wait the longest for the demanding spotlight in 'Serenade', memorably close to the end of the work. There is no doubt that the composer considered these matters carefully. The diarist Dika Newlin records, from a composition lesson in 1940, that Schoenberg 'named all the possible combinations of . . . instruments, and asked me to write them down and count them . . . He thinks it a good idea to list combinations in this way and thus have a better conception of your variety of resources. That is what he did for the instrumentation of *Pierrot lunaire*.'[7]

Most will agree with the impression of Alan Lessem, author of the important study *Music and Text in the Works of Arnold Schoenberg: The Critical Years 1908–1922*, that 'on the whole instrumental textures tend to become fuller as the work progresses' and that 'the piano is the leading [instrumental] protagonist of the melodramas.'[8] The piano was always going to be the backbone of the instrumental sound, drawing on Schoenberg's deep experience in solo and song composition. How other textural structures emerged is, in detail, a matter for conjecture. There are some examples of instrumental 'word painting', such as the 'pallid' *ppp* sound of flute, clarinet and muted violin to begin 'Eine blasse Wäscherin'. Similarly, in 'Raub' the 'redly gleaming princely rubies' are portrayed by the wind/string texture – we have Schoenberg's own word for this feature (cf. p. 18 above). Dripping in allusion and imagery though the *Pierrot* poems are, however, there was relatively little to tempt the composer to overindulge in pictorialism: where Schoenberg does 'indulge' (see, for example, discussion of 'Heimfahrt', pp. 70–1 below) it is in bold relief.

From the point of view of instrumentation, the spirit of distance, or alienation, that imbues *Pierrot* is carried through logically. Schoenberg avoids any frank instrumental exoticism – that is, he avoids using, say, a harmonium (as in *Herzgewächse*), a saxophone, or a range of percussion instruments. The challenge was to make new sounds from traditional resources. Literalism, too, is often avoided. On a hand-written copy of the poems, probably at a very early stage in his musings, next to the word '*Riesenbogen*' (giant bow) in 'Serenade', he made a note, 'Violincello Solo',[9] just a few words away from the instrument mentioned in 'Pierrot scrapes on his viola' – which instrument is actually available in the ensemble, and which plays only a few minutes earlier in No. 17. Schoenberg conceives of a monstrous viola, not a real one. Nor is there 'pizzicato' in the music at that word in the next line of the text. Nor, when Pierrot 'throws aside' the viola, does the cello stop playing: on the contrary, it seems to assert a momentary and ghastly animation of the inanimate (see Ex. 2).

Relatively little information is available about events preceding the premiere. We know that Schoenberg made a fair copy of each item as it was finished for the pianist Eduard Steuermann to use in coaching Zehme. On 2 October 1912 Schoenberg wrote to Zemlinsky that he had held twenty-five general rehearsals, and that the premier on 16 October would go very well,[10] as it clearly did. Three public performances took place in the small Choralion Hall, to full houses consisting mainly of professional musicians, and critics:

Dark screens stood on the stage, and between them was Albertine Zehme in the costume of Colombine. Behind the scenes a handful of musicians conducted by Schoenberg played ... The performance – to the astonishment of the critics – resulted in an ovation for Schoenberg. The greater part of the audience remained in the hall after the end of the performance and forced a repeat.[11]

Schoenberg was legendary in his lifetime for his sheer speed of composition, and he repeatedly encouraged this reputation:

I composed three-fourths of both the second and the fourth movements of my Second String Quartet in one-and-a-half days each. I completed the half-hour music of my opera *Erwartung* in fourteen days. Several times I wrote two or three pieces of *Pierrot lunaire* and the song-cycle *Hängende Gärten* [*sic*] in a day. I could mention many more such examples.[12]

Ex. 2: 'Serenade', bars 35–6

Although there is nothing insincere here, such claims clearly suited Schoenberg's campaign to oppose the equally legendary image of labouring cerebralism, which was so often used in the vituperative criticism he faced throughout his life. Whenever, in his lectures, journals and more formal writings, he could with integrity use the word 'inspiration', he did so. This must not be allowed to cloud, as it often does in offhand commentary on the genesis, the clear picture of hard work and relatively protracted thought that emerges from the surviving evidence – even if, as discussed in the preceding chapter, Schoenberg was in a general sense cocked and loaded for his task. No. 9, the first melodrama to be begun, was also finished on the same day. No. 3 came next, begun on 1 April, finished the next day. There was then a break, and No. 1, begun on 17 April, was not completed until 29 April, during which time six more melodramas were started of which four were completed. 'Crosses', No. 14, one of the key melodramas in many respects – but tiny compared with some of the items Schoenberg mentions in the comment above – took a great deal of time, from 27 April until 9 July. There is also evidence of detailed abandoned work. One sketch shows the attempt to combine twelve fragments (see p. 57 below). There remained, indeed, a mass of unfinished business in Schoenberg's compositional archive, from the smallest ideas to the largest projects (especially *Moses und Aron*, worked on during his last two decades, Act III of which was barely begun when he died in 1951).

Rather than concentrate on rapidity or otherwise in the genesis of *Pierrot*, we do better to note the renewed confidence and decisiveness that steered Schoenberg through the fertile spring and summer of 1912. What amazes is the surety with which possibilities became certainties. The historian, following in Schoenberg's footsteps, can try to imagine, armed with knowledge of the composer's previous achievements, how he came up with this or that potential material; but his ability to draw the line, to decide 'this is finished', is beyond explanation. The known historical records of the genesis of *Pierrot* – because of the apparent compositional experimentation, and its potential for creative catastrophe – are exemplary of what Schoenberg called 'vision'. Once we have the score of *Pierrot*, we can see that it could not have been otherwise. Schoenberg saw it through on a wing and a prayer. Perhaps it is only right that this work, as not only the solar plexus but also the 'mind' (Stravinsky) of early twentieth-century music, should show its fragile origins in its creation. Pierrot just popped in to twentieth-century culture opportunistically, long to remain there, as we have seen. It is surely ironic that he should have 'chosen' Schoenberg, who thus embraced a real threat to his tortured middle age and to his compositional career, as Wellesz sensed in his pioneering book:

I am to some extent distrustful of people who know only *Pierrot lunaire*, and admire Schoenberg on the strength of this one work, without troubling to know his other compositions. Such an admiration seeks out from the treasures of a composer of genius the particular work that may have a certain effect on even an unpractised hearer, without considering that *Pierrot lunaire* represents only a single link in a chain of which all the other links are of equal value.[13]

And it is true that *Pierrot* invites the kind of concentrated and to some extent insulated study which is the subject of the following chapter. No doubt Schoenberg's reputation will survive it.

4

'Pierrot lunaire'

In this chapter each melodrama of *Pierrot* is discussed in turn. Each discussion begins with translations of Schoenberg's note of instrumentation and tempo designation, the text and Andrew Porter's elegant English translation, and each ends with a note of the composer's instruction for the timing between items.

There are a number of recurring topics in what follows. Above all, repeated comment is made on the 'tonality' of Schoenberg's music in *Pierrot*. However, some of the melodramas are best understood – beyond the confines of elaborate, music-theoretic description that would be inappropriate here – as thematic structures. The immediate formal articulation of the musical surface is often our best guide to an appreciation of the effect *Pierrot* has in performance. Various other general matters, such as the syllabicism of the *Sprechstimme* settings, the degree of 'cyclicity' in Op. 21, the techniques of musical contrast, and word-music relations, are allowed to arise at pertinent points of the individual considerations; and thus attention is drawn from time to time to the wider focus of the whole work.

One recurring topic may be thought idiosyncratic – what is called here the 'principal rhythm' of seven equally spaced notes (or chords). From the point of view of technical analysis, the pitch-motivic curve described by the principal rhythm in No. 1 and elsewhere (for example the bass clarinet entry in No. 5, bar 32), rather than just the rhythmic figure, may seem to be the proper focus of attention. Although there is without doubt pitch-motivic reference of this kind in *Pierrot*, it was the rhythmic motive itself that preoccupied Schoenberg compositionally, a flexible musical 'idea' to be resorted to again and again in the melodramas: it could be repeated, expanded, contracted, added to, truncated, counterpointed against itself, and – what is most important - set either to repeated pitches or to any number of pitch 'shapes'. There is no authority in Schoenberg's own writings for making the claim that an all-important rhythmic element is pervasive in *Pierrot*; nevertheless, the work itself offers this claim to us whether as close students of the score or eager members of an audience.

PART I

1 Mondestrunken   Moondrunk

[flute, violin, piano, later with cello: with movement]

Den Wein, den man mit Augen trinkt,	The wine that through the eyes is drunk,
Giesst Nachts der Mond in Wogen nieder,	at night the moon pours down in torrents,
Und eine Springflut überschwemmt	until a spring-flood overflows
Den stillen Horizont.	the silent far horizon.
Gelüste, schauerlich und süss,	Desires, shuddering and sweet,
Durchschwimmen ohne Zahl die Fluten!	are swimming through the flood unnumbered!
Den Wein, den man mit Augen trinkt,	The wine that through the eyes is drunk,
Giesst Nachts der Mond in Wogen nieder.	at night the moon pours down in torrents.
Der Dichter, den die Andacht treibt,	The poet, whom devotion drives,
Berauscht sich an dem heilgen Tranke,	grows tipsy on the sacred liquor,
Gen Himmel wendet er verzückt	to heaven turning his enraptured gaze
Das Haupt und taumeld saugt und schlürft er	and reeling, sucks and slurps up
Den Wein, den man mit Augen trinkt.	the wine that through the eyes is drunk.

The first melodrama was begun and completed early in Schoenberg's work on *Pierrot*, with his ideas for the cycle already, however, well thought through. In *Pierrot*'s final form, 'Mondestrunken' is a crucial exposition of mood and musical material. Many of the consistent hallmarks of the cycle are first presented here.

The initial piano ostinato (see Ex. 3) uses the principal rhythm of *Pierrot*. The musical control exerted by the instruments, rather than the voice, is revealed in the fragmentary interludes: at bar 7, with sudden loud dynamics; at bar 15 where the second verse begins, musically, with an *a tempo* and new texture; at bars 27–8 which close the second verse; and in the abrupt, non-cadential ending at bar 39. The instrumental control is also evident in the overall canvas here, marked especially by the late entry of the cello at bar 29, doubling the piano in its tenor register, flagging the announcement of the 'poet', the first being to enter the text.

Such densely chromatic harmony is best understood as a balance of factors. First, references to major–minor tonality are undoubtedly active in

Ex. 3: 'Mondestrunken', bars 1–7

various parts of *Pierrot*, and will be discussed in later contexts where they are much more evident than in 'Mondestrunken'. Secondly, there are absolute pitch relationships – for example, many quasi-cadential points in *Pierrot* seem to focus around the note E and its chromatic neighbours. Third is the factor of the total chromatic, an intuitive, or largely intuitive sense common to many composers in this period of the harmonic boundary provided by the interplay of all twelve pitch classes.[1] The opening of *Pierrot* is a typical instance. Piano, violin and flute together use ten of the twelve pitch classes. The 'missing' ones are B and F, B 'supplied' by the first downbeat of the recitation (though we cannot assume that the *Sprechstimme* of any particular performance will actually convey the note B), and F supplied, and supported in the piano part, at the next focal downbeat in bar 6 (cf. Ex. 3 above).

The recitation itself in this melodrama is also expositional in many respects. The vocal tessitura, as far as the notated pitch actually matters, covers nearly two octaves (A-F#) and moves rapidly across this range. The setting is syllabic and, as will be generally the case in *Pierrot*, moves through the text rapidly, so that the clarifying repetitions, especially the double repetitions of line 1 at line 7 and at the closing line 13, are weighty articulations of the mood of each melodrama. The 'syllabicism' of *Pierrot* is among its most memorable features. Syllabicism is, moreover, a virtually unavoidable consequence of the use of *Sprechstimme*, for melisma without discrete pitches can be achieved only by glissando, which is a slender resource. However, it has to be borne in mind that Schoenberg was exceptionally sparing with vocal melisma throughout his career. Rather than thinking of *Sprechstimme* as a cause of the syllabicism in *Pierrot*, it is probably more accurate to assume that Schoenberg's syllabicism was a compositional habit that had primed him with a felicitous approach to the challenges of devising a sustained musical recitation.

Textually, 'Mondestrunken' immediately opens up the world of the impossible, of intoxication by a wine which comes out at night, that is, moonlight; of sacramental slurping; and of desires which are 'schauerlich und süss', literally, 'horrible and sweet'. This fantasy world of irreconcilability is writ slightly larger in the contrast between the torrid 'Mondestrunken' and the cool 'Colombine'.

(. . . ample pause, as if in time)
2 Colombine   Columbine

[violin, piano, later with flute and clarinet in A: flowing]

Des Mondlichts bleiche Blüten,	The moonlight's pallid blossoms,
Die weissen Wunderrosen,	the white and wondrous roses,
Blühn in den Julinächten –	bloom in July's nights –
O bräch ich eine nur!	oh, could I pluck but one!
Mein banges Leid zu lindern,	My heavy load to lighten,
Such ich am dunklen Strome	in darkling streams I search for
Des Mondlichts bleiche Blüten,	the moonlight's pallid blossoms,
Die weissen Wunderrosen.	the white and wondrous roses.
Gestillt wär all mein Sehnen,	Then stilled were all my yearning,
Dürft ich so märchenheimlich,	could I, as in a fable,
So selig leis – entblättern	so tenderly – but scatter
Auf deine braunen Haare	upon your brown tresses
Des Mondlichts bleiche Blüten!	the moonlight's pallid blossoms!

There are a variety of generic references in *Pierrot*. If it is hard to discern any in No. 1, it should be no surprise that the contrasting 'Colombine' is instantly recognizable in its genre – it begins as a waltz, at the opening, for violin (muted) and piano. Similarly, however hard it may be to identify a clear-cut form in 'Mondestrunken', the second melodrama falls neatly into alternating sections (violin bars 1–5, piano bars 6–11/12, violin bars 13–17, piano bars 18–20), then what Schoenberg would have called a 'liquidation' in which thematic and rhythmic continuity breaks down,[2] and a coda in which flute and clarinet join the piano to provide an ostinato accompaniment to the violin melody. The principal rhythm is represented mainly by the development of its three-note anacrusis, with which this number also closes.

Some of the formal clarity introduced in No. 2 can be assessed by comparing the treatment of the twice-repeated first line of text. In 'Mondestrunken' the dead-pan rhythm of the opening is varied in the middle, and this middle version is augmented at the end (see bars 2–4, 23–4, 36–8). In 'Colombine', rhythmic identity ties together the whole number (see Ex. 4).

Although in the subsequent melodramas there is often a close rhythmic kinship in the settings of first, seventh and thirteenth lines (especially in

Ex. 4: 'Colombine', *Sprechstimme*, bars 1–3, 21–3 and 35–8

Nos. 18 and 20), nowhere else in *Pierrot* is the correspondence as perceptibly precise as in No. 2.

(. . . ample pause)

3 Der Dandy   The Dandy

[piccolo, clarinet in A, piano: fast]

Mit einem phantastischen Lichtstrahl	And with a fantastical light-beam
Erleuchtet der Mond die krystallnen Flakons	the moon sheds a light on the crystalline flask
Auf dem schwarzen, hochheiligen Waschtisch	on the ebony, highly sacred washstand
Des schweigenden Dandys von Bergamo.	of the taciturn dandy from Bergamo.
In tönender, bronzener Schale	In sonorous, bronzen basin
Lacht hell die Fontäne, metallischen Klangs.	laughs brightly the fountain's metallical cry.
Mit einem phantastischen Lichtstrahl	And with a fantastical light-beam
Erleuchtet der Mond die krystallnen Flakons.	the moon sheds a light on the crystalline flask.
Pierrot mit dem wächsernem Antlitz	Pierrot with waxen complexion
Steht sinnend and denkt: wie er heute sich schminkt?	stands musing and thinks: what makeup for today?
Fort schiebt er das Rot und des Orients Grün	Rejecting the red and the orient green

Und bemalt sein Gesicht in erhabenem   he bedizens his face in a high noble style
  Stil
Mit einem phantastischen Mondstrahl.   with a fantastical moonbeam.

Schoenberg's masterful organization of the poems is at least as striking here as elsewhere. In No. 3 Pierrot himself is named, and it is at this stage that we might consider the drama of identity set off by 'Der Dandy'. The naming of Pierrot here helps to orientate the audience, but what is given is taken away, for a puzzle is brought to the fore. Is the reciter Pierrot? It was a puzzle from the outset anyway, for Pierrot is a male. So who is the reciter, if not Pierrot? To the extent that the reciter does take on an identity, it may well be that of Columbine, and this is how Zehme was costumed in the premiere. She is present, perhaps in the first person, in No. 2 (though she mentions 'your' brown hair in line 12), and will be again in No. 5, in No. 6 where the Madonna appears as perhaps the only sympathetically, and probably sororially treated character, briefly in No. 7, in No. 9, 'Gebet an Pierrot', and in the closing 'O alter Duft'. In the recent commentary of Glen Watkins (see above, p. 23) we are told that 'even in the potentially touching homecoming of the last piece Pierrot confesses to ["a merry troupe of roguish pranks"] and befuddled senses';[3] yet it is only supposition that the 'I' of No. 21 is Pierrot himself, after the repeated third-person reference to his exploits, starting here in No. 3 and finishing in the penultimate number. Elsewhere, rich seams of meaning will remain unmined if we do not constantly hear Columbine's, or at least the narrator's, own independent voice – as, for instance, supplicant in No. 9, and avenger in No. 12. The matter is not clear-cut, and this is Schoenberg's point in his selection and ordering of the poems. Whereas in *Erwartung* the protagonist, the main character, is a mysterious singer, with no name, and hardly any identification, in *Pierrot* there is no protagonist at all, no lucid relationship between the focus of attention, the woman reciter, and the focus of textual attention, Pierrot himself.

'Der Dandy' offers more sustained melody than in the first two songs, especially in the clarinet, which at one point (bars 18–20) lulls the voice almost into song (the composer writes here: 'nearly sung, with a touch of melodiousness, very drawn out, to match the clarinet'; and four notes in bar 16 are, literally, 'sung'). At precisely the point where Pierrot's name is first mentioned, bar 21,[4] the piano plays in octaves for the first time in the work, to uncanny effect (see Ex. 5). One must suspect that this snatch of melody is a quotation, though no commentator seems to have identified it.

Ex. 5: 'Der Dandy', bars 21–3

In view of the lyrical tone introduced in 'Der Dandy', Rosen's comment on its pitch-structure is particularly provocative:

> In the third piece of *Pierrot lunaire* . . . the clarinet part could be transposed a half-step up or down while the other instruments remain at the correct pitch, and (although some effect would be lost) the music would still make sense; but if the dynamics are not respected, the music becomes totally absurd and makes no sense at all. The harmonic content of the piece is conveyed less through the simultaneous chords of the instruments playing together than by the individual lines described by each instrument. That occurs . . . because the relationship of dissonance has been partially displaced from the interval or the chord on to other aspects of music.[5]

It is true that to transpose the clarinet would produce a number of brief doublings with the piano and piccolo. Yet it is also true that there are in any case such passing doublings in the score as it stands (e.g. bars 3, D#, and 9, A). On two counts, however, Rosen's comment has to be taken with a grain of salt. First, there are various points at which the clarinet supplies pitch classes which contribute to filling up the total chromatic (a process discussed above at the opening of 'Mondestrunken'), and the loss of this effect would surely damage our impression of the richness of Schoenberg's harmony. Secondly, such an interval as the shrieking perfect fourth (E♭ to A♭) on the first downbeat cannot be replaced (by a tritone or major third) without radical damage: this is equally true of the F/E octaves between piccolo and clarinet in the last bar. It must also be borne in mind that Schoenberg's conception of *Pierrot* was crystal clear, nor did he tamper with the score in his painstaking rehearsals for the premiere, a point remarked upon in a memoir of Eduard Steuermann, a Schoenberg pupil and the first pianist to play in *Pierrot*.[6]

(. . . shortest possible pause)

4 Eine blasse Wäscherin	A Pallid Laundrymaid

[flute, clarinet in A, violin: flowing, but with many changes of tempo]

Eine blasse Wäscherin	See a pallid laundrymaid
Wäscht zur Nachtzeit bleiche Tücher,	washing nightly faded linen;
Nackte, silberweisse Arme	naked, silver-whitish arms
Streckt sie nieder in die Flut.	stretching downward in the flood.
Durch die Lichtung schleichen Winde,	Through the clearing gentle breezes
Leis bewegen sie den Strom.	lightly ruffle up the stream.
Eine blasse Wäscherin	See a pallid laundrymaid
Wäscht zur Nachtzeit bleiche Tücher.	washing nightly faded linen.

Ex. 6: 'Eine blasse Wäscherin', bars 1–6

Und die sanfte Magd des Himmels,	And the tender maid of heaven,
Von den Zweigen zart umschmeichelt,	by the branches softly fondled,
Breitet auf die dunklen Wiesen	lays out on the darkling meadows
Ihre lichtgewobnen Linnen –	all her linen woven of moonbeams -
Eine blasse Wäscherin.	see a pallid laundrymaid.

Each of the opening three numbers has been musically, and vocally, jagged. We now witness a still cameo, not so much bloodless as bled dry. Flute, clarinet and violin are instructed to play 'with completely equal volume [*ppp*], without any expression', and the recitation 'should be like an accompaniment to the instruments throughout'. The piano is silent.

In the early part of this number there is what came to be called in German musical circles around this period a *Klangfarbenmelodie* (sound-colour melody), in which the part-writing does not correspond to the voice-leading (see Ex. 6).[7] This makes later, explicit, linear ideas all the more prominent, for example the descending lines in bars 12 and 13 (in the first three notes of the principal rhythm, which was given in full in bar 6: see Ex. 7). These little descents are shown for the obvious reason that they make references to major–minor tonality, and this is a characteristic of the whole laundrymaid scene. The references work at different levels. On the one hand, Schoenberg uses mainly fourth/fifth-based harmony here, so that even 'dissonant' chords have an element of tonal stability – as, for example, in bar 14. And of course bar 4 (see above) sets the audience on the track of 'tonal' listening with the first unambiguous triads of *Pierrot*. On the other hand, there is a deeper tonal 'feel' to this music, which may seem to prolong a sonority based on D at the opening, and which certainly ends 'in' G minor,

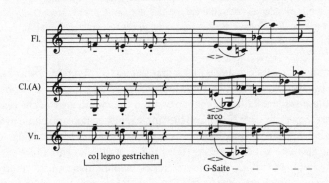

Ex. 7: 'Eine blasse Wäscherin', bars 12–13, instrumental parts

with the chord Bb, G, A, D (reading upwards) sounding four times. In the composer's own understanding, 'Eine blasse Wäscherin' probably counted as a tonal piece. His comments in the essay 'Problems of Harmony' (1934) seem to be illustrated by it precisely:

> We can take [complicated chords] that in no manner refer to a key, and join them to diatonic triads, and similar successions, in this manner creating, *a posteriori*, an impression that the preceding dissonances, no matter how unprepared and unresolved, referred to this key . . . One thing is certain: all chords, that in any way turn to a key, no matter how dissonant they may be, fall within the domain of the old harmony and do not disturb tonality.[8]

(continue immediately without any pause)

5 Valse de Chopin   Valse de Chopin

[flute, clarinet in A (later bass clarinet in Bb, piano: slow waltz]

Wie ein blasser Tropfen Bluts	As a pallid drop of blood
Färbt die Lippen einer Kranken,	stains the lips of a consumptive,
Also ruht auf diesen Tönen	so there lurks within this music
Ein vernichtungssüchtiger Reiz.	morbid soul-destructive charm.
Wilder Lust Akkorde stören	Wild accords of passion
Der Verzweiflung eisgen Traum –	breaking desperation's icy dream
Wie ein blasser Tropfen Bluts	as a pallid drop of blood
Färbt die Lippen einer Kranken.	stains the lips of a consumptive.
Heiss and jauchzend, süss und	Fierce, triumphant, sweet and yearning,
schmachtend,	
Melancholisch düstrer Walzer,	melancholy sombre waltzing,
Kommst mir nimmer aus den Sinnen!	you will never leave my senses,
Haftest mir an den Gedanken,	cling to each thought as I think it,
Wie ein blasser Tropfen Bluts!	as a pallid drop of blood!

Porter surely invites censure with his translation 'consumptive', where the German says merely 'sick'. He introduces too much of Chopin. Schoenberg seems to introduce little Chopin, apart from the overall style of the piano part (see especially bars 27–9), and the single repeated note transition to the next item, which is as Chopinesque as any post-tonal composer could make such a gesture. Yet Schoenberg does put himself into this number, in response to the lines 'so there lurks within this music morbid soul-destructive charm' (see Ex. 8). For all that this correspondence cannot be sustained analytically (for example, it would be better scholarly protocol

Ex. 8: 'Valse de Chopin' bars 14–16 and No. 4 of Six Little Piano Pieces,
Op. 19 (opening bars)

to relate the piano melody of bars 14–16 to the 'Des Mondlichts bleiche Blüten' rhythm of No. 2), the quadruple cue – text, instrument, parody, historical awareness – is of substance.

'Valse de Chopin' is close to 'Colombine' in style, though the bass clarinet (from bar 32, after 'melancholy' in bar 30), which repeats two of its lowest playable notes and uses not only the principal rhythm, but also an inversion of the opening piano figure of No. 1, is a marker of the macabre events to unfold. Most listeners will probably have the impression that the instrumental texture here is more complex than before, and there is a repeated saturation of the total chromatic, so that triads, of which there are many, are hardly heard as such. Even if the source of Schoenberg's ability to generate these dense harmonic structures must remain a mystery, at least we can observe some of the balancing compositional control which doubtless contributes to the overall coherence of the musical language. There is a varied but clear reprise providing orientation in the middle (compare bars 23ff. with the opening); and an overall shape is imposed by the reduced tempo after the climax (bars 28ff.), an effect that is much more pronounced here than in 'Der Dandy'.[9] What may be found more interesting is the patterning of the bass line. For example, between bars 9 and 14 the piano's lowest notes descend by chromatic step from D to G, and in the climactic bars there are fourth- (B, F, C, bar 27), whole-tone- (C#, B,

A, bar 28) and fifth-progressions (F# in bar 29 to C# on the following downbeat). This kind of patterning is a substitute for functional harmony, of which the composer was fully conscious. Writing of such patterns in general, he noted that 'it is obvious why such a progression has a convincing and logical effect: because the succession of tones works according to a clear, comprehensible rule'.[10]

With No. 5 we have in fact entered into a later stage of the overall forging of *Pierrot*, for it was the thirteenth melodrama to be started in Schoenberg's manuscript (7 May 1912). He had already begun work on some of the most substantial items destined, eventually, for Part III – 'Serenade', 'Gemeinheit' and 'Heimweh' – whereas what eventually became Nos. 1–4 were drafted during the first three weeks of April. Those who detect a broadening of compositional vision in 'Valse de Chopin' can thus point to a suggestive chronology, of which much more will be said in discussion of Parts II and III.

(continue without a pause)

6 Madonna   Madonna

[flute, bass clarinet in B♭, violin, later with cello and piano: moderate tempo]

Steig, o Mutter aller Schmerzen,	Rise, O Mother of all Sorrows,
Auf den Altar meiner Verse!	on the altar of my verses!
Blut aus deinen magern Brüsten	Blood pours forth from withered bosom
Hat des Schwertes Wut vergossen.	where the cruel sword has pierced it.
Deine ewig frischen Wunden	And thine ever-bleeding wounds
Gleichen Augen, rot und offen.	seem like eyes, red and open.
Steig, o Mutter aller Schmerzen,	Rise, O Mother of all Sorrows
Auf den Altar meiner Verse!	on the altar of my verses!
In den abgezehrten Händen	In thy torn and wasted hands
Hältst du deines Sohnes Leiche,	holding thy Son's holy body,
Ihn zu zeigen aller Menschheit –	thou revealst Him to all mankind –
Doch der Blick der Menschen meidet	but the eyes of men are turned away,
Dich, o Mutter aller Schmerzen!	O Mother of all Sorrows!

Flute and bass clarinet play subdued, intertwining melodies against pizzicato cello 'scales' ascending and descending – all the gestures, but not the pitches, of a Baroque 'religioso' (we might be reminded of a piece such as Bach's Prelude in B minor from the Well-Tempered Clavier, Book 1), which the recitation matches in its stylized word-setting of plodding quavers (bars 2^3–4, 5–6). A 'liquidation' (see p. 33 above) from bar 7 breaks down this effect and leads to a satirical, even sarcastic repetition of the opening lines (bars 10–12) where the voice is now 'very high' and *ppp*, suggesting a squeaking intonation of the solemn entreaty. So far in *Pierrot* the music has been more or less continuous (the opening of No. 4 being the first clear exception), and this reinforces the dramatic impact of the silences which set the scene for the febrile third verse of 'Madonna' (see Ex. 9). The drama is completed by the crashing entry of the piano at bar 21. The design

Ex. 9: 'Madonna', bars 12–16

has great impact: we surely expect No. 6, for one string and two woodwind instruments, to proceed without piano, as did No. 4 with its similar combination. Schoenberg follows through the plan, after the 'massive' (*'wuchtig'*) climax of No. 6, by closing the first part of *Pierrot* with a number for flute and voice alone.

The introduction of religious parody launches the narrative of *Pierrot* out of the relatively subdued imagery of the first five poems. The audience has been soothed, not only poetically, but musically, into a pale, shallow and, in 'Valse de Chopin', rather skittish disposition. The last nine bars of 'Madonna' are a jolt indeed. They also have the potential to cause offence, as Schoenberg noted in a letter of 30 December 1922:

> In Geneva and Amsterdam I notice for the first time that 'Madonna', 'Red Mass' and also 'Crosses' somehow give religious offence. Such a possibility never before crossed my mind and nothing was ever further from me in all my life than any such intention . . . I seem to have had an altogether much naiver view of these poems than most people have . . . Anyway I am not responsible for what people make up their minds to read into the words. If they were musical, not a single one of them, would give a damn for the words. Instead, they would go away whistling the tunes.[11]

What has been called this 'characteristic outburst'[12] rather ducks the issue perhaps, for to not 'give a damn for the words' would be to contradict Schoenberg's own, later, stated position: 'songs, operas and oratorios would not exist if music were not added to heighten the expression of their text.'[13] Given the topics of extreme, ritualistic violence and punishment that imbue the seven poems Schoenberg selected for Part II, sacrilege is an inevitable component of *Pierrot*. People are quite likely to 'make up their minds to read' it into No. 6. Its appearance is an artistic necessity, and it is Schoenberg's impatience with those of the public who could not understand this creative imperative that best explains his comments.

(. . . fairly long pause)

7 Der kranke Mond	The Sick Moon

[flute: very slow beat]

Du nächtig todeskranker Mond	O sombre deathly-stricken moon
Dort auf des Himmels schwarzem Pfühl,	lying on heaven's dusky pillow
Dein Blick, so fiebernd übergross,	your stare, so wide-eyed, feverish,
Bannt mich wie fremde Melodie.	charms me, like far-off melody.
An unstillbarem Liebesleid	Of unappeasable pain of love

Stirbst du, an Sehnsucht, tief erstickt,	you die, of yearning, choked to death.
Du nächtig todeskranker Mond	O sombre deathly-stricken moon
Dort auf des Himmels schwarzem Pfühl.	lying on heaven's dusky pillow.

Den Liebsten, der im Sinnenrausch	The lover, with his heart aflame,
Gedankenlos zur Liebsten schleicht,	who heedless goes to meet his love,
Belustigt deiner Strahlen Spiel –	rejoices in your play of light,
Dein bleiches, qualgebornes Blut,	your pallid, pain-begotten blood,
Du nächtig todeskranker Mond.	O sombre deathly-stricken moon!

No. 7 is one of the melodramas that Schoenberg appears to have completed in one day, on 18 April. The solo flute begins with three long notes that presage the opening of Part II (probably composed subsequently, though this cannot be proved from the sources), followed by a version of the principal rhythm echoing, in slow motion, the main piano motive of 'Der Dandy' (e.g. bars 4–5, 11). Semiquaver figuration follows, reminiscent of much of the allegro material in previous numbers, and a rhapsodic elaboration continues into the third verse. A sense of 'formlessness' is arrested towards the end, not only by the motivic repetitions in the flute across bars 22–24, but by the unprecedented repetitions of the *Sprechstimme* (see Ex. 10). Increasingly, Schoenberg will draw the notated pitches of the recitation into the compositional process, and the end of 'Der kranke Mond' heralds this specificity. As will be discussed below, the compositional freedom of this number is not a sign of happenstance, for it was to these precise notes that the composer turned when making a paraphrase that would form the transition between Nos. 13 and 14. 'Der kranke Mond' does, however, highlight some of the difficulties of *Pierrot*, as the following excerpt from William Austin's extensive discussion, mentioned in chapter 3, illustrates:

In the instrumental parts of *Pierrot* and other mature works of Schoenberg, many passages resemble *Sprechstimme* in their elusive, wailing character. Some parts of the flute accompaniment in *The Sick Moon* exhibit this character: the flurries of sixteenth notes especially; the written intervals cannot be heard distinctly at such speed . . . In [bars] 15–16, the flute is to begin *pppp*, and then become much softer. What can this mean? . . . How can a performer decide whether the bar-lines signify accents and where not? How can a listener grasp the rhythms without following the score?[14]

The cyclic design of Part I clearly involves the return of the moon from No. 1 in No. 7. It is also clear that the quiet lassitude of No. 7 is a foil for the dramatic crisis unleashed in 'Madonna'. But at this stage of *Pierrot*,

Ex. 10: 'Der kranke Mond', bars 24–7

there is still plenty of humour in the air:

[Schoenberg tried] to get the speaker away from the tragic-heroine expression she was inclined to assume; he would step behind her when 'Der kranke Mond' became too tearful, saying in the rhythm of her speech, 'Don't despair, Mrs Zehme, don't despair; there is such a thing as life insurance!'[15]

PART II

8 Nacht (Passacaglia)   Night (Passacaglia)

[bass clarinet in B♭, cello, piano: with movement]

Finstre, schwarze Riesenfalter	Black gigantic butterflies
Töteten der Sonne Glanz.	have blotted out the shining sun.
Ein geschlossnes Zauberbuch,	Like a sorcerer's sealed book,
Ruht der Horizont – verschwiegen.	the horizon sleeps in silence.
Aus dem Qualm verlorner Tiefen	From the murky depths forgotten
Steigt ein Duft, Erinnrung mordend!	vapours rise, to murder memory!
Finstre, schwarze Riesenfalter	Black gigantic butterflies
Töteten der Sonne Glanz.	have blotted out the shining sun.
Und vom Himmel erdenwärts	And from heaven toward the earth,
Senken sich mit schweren Schwingen	sinking down on heavy pinions,
Unsichtbar die Ungetüme	all unseen descend the monsters
Auf die Menschenherzen nieder . . .	to the hearts of men below here . . .
Finstre, schwarze Riesenfalter.	Black gigantic butterflies.

Through the text Schoenberg plunges us at the beginning of Part II into an altogether more discomforting atmosphere. Yet it is not only a matter of imagery, of the famed 'Finstre, schwarze Riesenfalter' (often translated, inaccurately and less piquantly than here, as 'giant black moths') who have lived on far beyond the term Giraud and Hartleben can have foreseen for them. Musically, a new heightening of expression is achieved. 'Nacht' is scored for bass clarinet, cello and piano, in a low tessitura which, though it rises in the middle, nevertheless sinks back at the end, with cello and piano on their lowest possible notes.[16] The tessitura of the recitation also reaches down continually, incorporating the main motive, E –G –E, below middle C, 'sung . . . if possible' in bar 10 (it also appears in the voice at pitch in bars 15–16, and in bar 23). Instrumental effects include fluttertongue for bass clarinet (bars 13ff.), cello *sul ponticello* (bars 12ff.), and a low, *fff*, pedalled tremolando for piano (bar 16) at the end of the second verse.

The opening gives some indication of the strange sound world (see Ex. 11). It also shows, as annotated, the beginning of the compositional process signalled by Schoenberg's subtitle 'Passacaglia'. Rosen claims that this piece 'develops entirely from a ten-note motif [see above, bass clarinet, bars 4–6[1]]: everything can be traced back easily to that kernel. The harmony implied by these motifs pervades the music completely: they are meant to give any work composed by this method an individual and characteristic sonority. The method is an old one, going back to Bach and even to the late-fifteenth-century Netherlandish composers'.[17] Most other commentators, rightly in my view, have seen 'Nacht' as based on the three-note main motive, which, in the words of the authoritative Stuckenschmidt, 'appears in a hundred variants, diminished in quaver and crotchet movement, in three-part chords with a fixed rhythmical arrangement, in contrapuntal and canonic forms, and mirrored in its retrograde inversion'.[18] To this ought to be added an appreciation of the contextual coherence, for the three-note figures recall the opening of the principal rhythm, which appears in its authentic seven-note form, implicitly at the very opening (where there are seven attacks, the last one delayed) and in the crotchet chromatic figure, explicitly in the quaver patterns developed from bar 12.

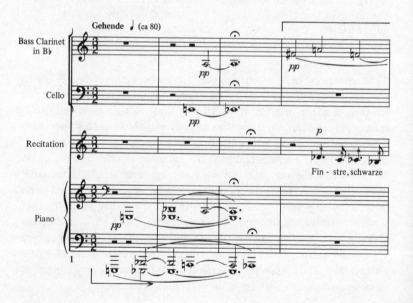

Ex. 11: 'Nacht', bars 1–8

49

'Nacht' has an intriguing genealogy, for the earliest sketch is of seven bars for voice and piano, with no indication of *Sprechstimme*. This may indicate an origin even before 12 March 1912, but possibly Schoenberg was contemplating at some stage a fully pitched contrapuntal set-piece to add to his armoury of compositional contrast. There are a number of further sketches for 'Nacht', and it shows signs of extensive revision even in the final manuscript.

(. . . very long pause, but quasi in tempo)

9 Gebet an Pierrot   Prayer to Pierrot

[clarinet in A, piano: moderate tempo]

Pierrot! Mein Lachen	Pierrot! my laughter
Hab ich verlernt!	have I unlearnt!
Das Bild des Glanzes	The dream of radiance
Zerfloss – Zerfloss!	dispersed, dispersed!
Schwarz weht die Flagge	Black waves the banner
Mir nun vom Mast.	upon the mast.
Pierrot! Mein Lachen	Pierrot! My laughter
Hab ich verlernt!	have I unlearned!
O gieb mir wieder,	O now return to me,
Rossarzt der Seele,	soul's veterinarian,
Schneemann der Lyrik,	Snowman of Lyric,
Durchlaucht vom Monde,	Your Lunar Highness,
Pierrot – mein Lachen!	Pierrot! - my laughter!

'Gebet an Pierrot' is a miniature between the large canvases of Nos. 8 and 10. It covers just over 20 bars, with brief rests punctuating some of the line-breaks in the recitation, and an overlapping of short instrumental ideas between piano and clarinet. The chromatic cell announced by the piano

Ex. 12: 'Gebet an Pierrot', bars 1–5, *Sprechstimme*

becomes the main pitch ingredient of this short setting, which derives much of its rhythmic detail from the principal rhythm (clarinet, bar 2).

Since 'Gebet an Pierrot' was almost certainly the first melodrama to be composed, it is worth examining a little of the craftsmanship with which Schoenberg responded to the text in what we know to have been a fever of compositional excitement (see Ex. 12). The parallelism between the first two motives leads to an anti-intonational stress on the last syllable of 'Lachen' ('my laugh*ter*'), neatly representing laughter itself. After this clipped opening the sustained setting of 'dream of radiance', with a melodic peak on the word 'Glanz', again illuminates the meaning, with the help of high and bright piano chords. The neutrality of the cadential 'zerfloss!' is truly 'dispersed!' when the word is repeated with a downwards interval, 'hissed' (*gezischt*). All this may seem to state the obvious, yet it is interesting that one can discuss the word-setting in such a traditional way – a sample confirmation of a point made in chapter 1 that the supporting generic type of Op. 21 is the song-cycle.

As the first melodrama (Schoenberg's initial gathering of eleven numbers was in the order 9, 5, 3, 2, 1, 11, 17, 7, 4, 13, 8) 'Gebet an Pierrot' would have had weighty textual significance overall. It would have animated both Pierrot and his supplicant Columbine from the start, with the straightforward accusation that Pierrot takes the fun out of life. In this sense at least, it can be surmised that Schoenberg chose to withhold 'Gebet an Pierrot' because it would have been far too clear and too serious as an opener. As No. 9, it fulfils the multiple functions that are easily seen in critical hindsight. Textually, it reintroduces Pierrot by name in part of a cumulative, if not systematic process – Pierrot is actually named in Nos. 3 (Part I), 9, 10, 11, 13 (Part II), and 15, 16, 17, 18, 19, 20 (Part III) – and brings some humour back to the vespertine afterglow of No. 8. It also casts Pierrot as a cause of loss, somewhat loftily, and thus gives a teasing, deceptive foretaste of the bloody necrolarceny of 'Raub'. Musically, 'Gebet an Pierrot' lacks the melodic, rhythmic, harmonic and textural richness of 'Mondestrunken', and that epic quality of No. 1 that is impossible to describe scientifically, but which earns it its priority in *Pierrot*.

(. . . no pause)

10 Raub	Theft

[flute, clarinet in A, violin, cello: moderate tempo]

Rote, fürstliche Rubine,	Redly gleaming princely rubies,
Blutge Tropfen alten Ruhmes,	bleeding drops of ancient glory

Schlummern in den Totenschreinen	slumber in the dead men's coffins,
Drunten in den Grabgewölben.	buried in the vaults below us.
Nachts, mit seine Zechkumpanen,	Nights, alone with his companions,
Steigt Pierrot hinab – zu rauben	Pierrot descends, to plunder
Rote, fürstliche Rubine,	redly gleaming princely rubies,
Blutge Tropfen alten Ruhmes.	bleeding drops of ancient glory.
Doch da – sträuben sich die Haare,	Then suddenly they're rooted,
Bleiche Furcht bannt sie am Platze:	scared to death, hair standing straight up:
Durch die Finsterniss – wie Augen! -	through the darkness, like eyes
Stieren aus den Totenschreinen	staring from the dead men's coffins –
Rote, fürstliche Rubine.	redly gleaming princely rubies.

The relatively unconstrained style of composition in 'Gebet an Pierrot', following the passacaglia, is continued here, although there is more clarity of formal shape. For instance, 'Raub' has an instrumental introduction (bars 1–4) and a postlude (bar 19), and the hint of symmetry is reinforced by ostinatos early and late on in the piece (bars 2–3 and 16–17). The recitation is subdued – the impression being that Schoenberg put his imagination to work mainly on the instruments in this number. The silence of the piano creates an instantly expectant air to the introduction, and a combination of flute, clarinet, and violin and cello both initially muted and struck *col legno*, promises new kinds of sound, while rehearsing some of the atmosphere of 'Eine blasse Wäscherin'. The string sounds change almost from bar to bar, arco to pizzicato, on the bridge to on the fingerboard, and to high harmonics in the second ostinato. In the woodwind the interplay of range and articulation is equally kaleidoscopic.

If this composition is in general 'unconstrained', 'Raub' is nevertheless one of those numbers in *Pierrot* where a degree of compositional systematization is in evidence – and, in this case, readily perceived. Although offering no sense of diatonic relationships, nor even of a vestigial tonality, it is striking in its harmonic coherence. This is because most of the simultaneities (not always literally 'chords') are formed from clusters of semitones. The closing chords in bar 19 illustrate this at its simplest (Fl.–D, Cl.–C#, Vn.–C, Vc.–B, followed by Fl.–C#, Cl.–C, Vn.–B, Vc.–Bb). This cannot explain how Schoenberg contemplated the actual connection or distribution of pitch levels throughout the piece, but it does tell us something about the harmonic continuity that supports prodigious timbral diversity. We can also be sure that in this case Schoenberg was clinically aware of the procedure, for the one-bar transition leaves no doubt: this composer could not as it were inadvertently bring in the piano on yet another four-note semitone cluster (A, B♭, B, C) or end the bar with a C# followed by three ascending minor ninths.

No. 11, 'Rote Messe', was completed about six weeks before 'Raub', thus the need for a transition arose immediately Schoenberg decided to place Nos. 10 and 11 in that order. He had no choice but to write it for piano: three of the other players must rapidly swap instruments (to piccolo, bass clarinet and viola), and the cellist needs a moment to remove the mute. But in any case the piano interlude leads enticingly into the arabesques of 'Rote Messe.

(. . . no pause)

11 Rote Messe	Red Mass

[piano, piccolo, bass clarinet in B♭, viola, cello: moderate tempo]

Zu grausem Abendmahle,	To gruesome grim communion,
Beim Blendeglanz des Goldes,	by blinding golden glitter,
Beim Flackerschein der Kerzen,	by flickering shine of candles,
Naht dem Altar – Pierrot!	comes to the altar – Pierrot!
Die Hand, die gottgeweihte,	His hand, to God devoted
Zerreisst die Priesterkleider	tears wide the priestly vestment,
Zu grausem Abendmahle,	At gruesome grim communion,
Beim Blendeglanz des Goldes.	by blinding golden glitter.
Mit segnender Geberde	He makes the sign of the cross
Zeigt er den bangen Seelen	blessing the trembling, trembling people,
Die triefend rote Hostie:	with trickling crimson wafer:
Sein Herz – in blutgen Fingern -	his heart in bloody fingers,
Zu grausem Abendmahle!	at gruesome grim communion.

As the adventure unfolds there seems to emerge in *Pierrot* an interaction of dramatic types, the 'cameo' (Anthony Payne, in his probing monograph on Schoenberg's principal compositions, put forward the idea that some of the *Pierrot* melodramas should be understood as what he calls 'single-process movements')[19] and the drama. There does not appear to be a consistent pattern in this respect, some grand design that would convince us of a quasi-operatic structure to Op. 21. It is nevertheless tempting to regard the end of Part I as projecting through the rest of the work a form of contrast that becomes active only cumulatively. In No. 6, 'Madonna', what was called the 'febrile' third verse reflects musically a dramatic revelation in the text, producing such a contrast within the melodrama as had beforehand (Nos. 1–6) been equalled only by the contrast between melodramas. This gives way to the 'cameo' of 'Der kranke Mond'. 'Nacht', 'Gebet an Pierrot' and 'Raub', for all their vivid characterization, do not seem to offer any kind of dramatic twist. Certainly this can be argued of 'Raub', with its fresco effect, to a text that could just as well have sustained the contrast and development of a big musical set-piece – there is actually more action suggested in the text of No. 11 than in, for example, the musically climactic 'Kreuze' with which Part II closes.

Those who agree that *Pierrot* offers an unsystematic but cumulative interplay of action and reflection will have little difficulty in regarding 'Rote Messe' as its apex, at the dramatic extreme from both No. 1 and No. 21, the finest cameo of all, 'O alter Duft'. It may be a fanciful double accounting to detect here a trace of Schoenberg's original bipartite plan – after ten numbers, the eleventh, and after twenty numbers (but including No. 11), the twenty-first. What is not at all fanciful is to bear in mind that in the composer's first gathering of eleven melodramas, 'Rote Messe' was the central one (see above, p. 51), its drama fully exposed between the stylized 'Mondestrunken' and 'Parodie'.

The three musical sections of 'Rote Messe' correspond to the verses. A high piano ostinato, pedalled and with trills, portrays the glitter, flicker and shine of the words, and inevitably reminds us of the very opening of *Pierrot*. This gives way to what is probably the most tumultuous storm of notes in the work so far – bar 12, for example, is not only *fff* in four instruments, but the five superimposed trills contain nine different pitches. In the third section, beginning at bar 18, it is, as so often in Schoenberg, the clarinet (here, bass clarinet) which restores a kind of terrifying lyricism. Once again we find a unity that balances the extreme contrasts of surface musical expression. For example, the rhythm of the opening piano arabesques, especially the feature of trills preceded by rapid anacrusis, is carried right through to the canonic outburst of bar 15. And, in a wider perspective, the piano presents a direct recall of its 'Mondestrunken' motive from No. 1 (left hand, bars 20–2) as Pierrot consummates this 'sacrilegious' red mass (see above, p. 44).

(. . . shortest possible pause)

12 Galgenlied	Gallows Song

[viola, cello, later with piccolo: very fast]

| Die dürre Dirne | The haggard harlot |
| Mit langem Halse | whose neck is scrawny |

Wird seine letzte	will be the last
Geliebte sein.	of his mistresses.
In seinem Hirne	And in his skull
Steckt wie ein Nagel	she'll stick like a needle,
Die dürre Dirne	the haggard harlot
Mit langem Halse.	whose neck is scrawny.
Schlank wie die Pinie,	Slim as a pine tree,
Am Hals ein Zöpfchen –	she has a pigtail,
Wollüstig wird sie	gaily she'll bind it
Den Schelm umhalsen,	around his neck,
Die dürre Dirne!	the haggard harlot!

'Galgenlied', on the other hand, is a relatively slight piece, 'aphoristic, ghostly, fleeting' in Stuckenschmidt's neat description.[20] As the reciter scampers through the text, viola and cello, then piccolo, scamper through a progressive rhythmic diminution, with crescendo and accelerando. Not only is this a cameo, but it is also a one-gesture piece, a musical wave of the hand, with which Schoenberg seems to have intended to complete his second gathering (according to Brinkmann).[21] It would have made a rousing finish, and it does serve its purpose as No. 12 by separating two dramatic pieces. However, 'Galgenlied' is a severe test of comprehensibility. Musically, it is a composition that proceeds rapidly and ends quickly to such a degree that it can disturb the audience's concentration: any listener would be forgiven for thinking 'what was that?' during the silence Schoenberg allows at the end. And it is as difficult for the reciter to enunciate the words as it is for those words to be understood. Yet these are ultimately matters of opinion. One might well take the more positive general view put forward by MacDonald: '[Schoenberg's] music will often demand complete attention and a quickness of mind to match its own, but with a little familiarity it will begin to establish itself in the listener's imaginative universe.'[22]

(. . . fairly long pause)

13 Enthauptung	Beheading

[bass clarinet in B♭, viola, cello, piano: fairly quick]

Der Mond, ein blankes Türkenschwert	The moon, a shining Turkish sword
Auf einem schwarzen Seidenkissen,	upon a black and silken cushion,
Gespenstisch gross – dräut er hinab	and spectral vast hangs like a threat
Durch schmerzensdunkle Nacht.	in sorrow-darkened night!

Ex. 13: 'Enthauptung', bars 1–5, cello

Pierrot irrt ohne Rast umher	Pierrot restlessly roams about
Und starrt empor in Todesängsten	and stares on high in deathly fear
Zum Mond, dem blanken Türkenschwert	at the moon, a shining Turkish sword
Auf einem schwarzen Seidenkissen.	upon a black and silken cushion.
Es schlottern unter ihm die Knie,	And shaking, quaking at the knees,
Ohnmächtig bricht er jäh zusammen.	oh, suddenly he faints, collapses,
Er wähnt: es sause strafend schon	convinced that there comes whistling down
Auf seinen Sünderhals hernieder	upon his sinful guilty neck
Der Mond, das blanke Türkenschwert.	the moon, a shining Turkish sword.

Schoenberg originally planned 'Enthauptung' as the penultimate number of the first gathering, and it retains some of that architectural function as the penultimate number of Part II, again, like No. 6 (Madonna) of Part I, providing a sense of dramatic peak before closure. The opening cello melody (see Ex. 13) leaves no doubt of the impassioned scenario that is to unfold here and in the next number, with which it is closely bound in various ways that are considered below.

At the end of the first verse (bar 10) the sharply accentuated rhythms give way to the beginning of a dense development in which eventually, at bar 13, five lines of semiquavers (including two on the piano) are interwoven in a welter of notes covering the total chromatic. It seems that Schoenberg wants to offer some kind of referential pitch control,[23] for the C/B dyad of the cello's first bar is sounded twice, *sff*, in the piano (bars 11 and 14), and once again forte at the end of bar 17. C is also to be the eventual goal of the bass (bar 21). There is also a powerful moment of clarification at the beginning of the third verse (bar 17), when the panchromatic 'welter' gives way to a bar's worth of hammered whole-tone chords in the piano (the other three instruments are also in a whole-tone relationship with each other). In such a context as this, the traditionally unstable whole-tone harmony takes on quite the opposite function, bringing stability at a point of formal demarcation.

The points of referentiality and clarification are important, for in some respects the middle section of 'Enthauptung' is the epitome of the kind of composing that drew so much critical fire towards Schoenberg. No amount of technical study of bars 10–16 seems, to this author, to reveal a pitch grammar of any kind, and one can well join Rosen (see p. 37 above) in thinking that the misreading of one instrument by a semitone or so would make little real difference to the overall effect. It has the appearance of being the kind of composing anyone might do, and thus has the potential to rattle the critics beyond endurance: 'how *dare* Schoenberg do this?' – the press-book anthology overflows with such sentiments.[24] But only Schoenberg could do it in 1912, and its artistic effect is undeniable: by the standards of complexity that have become familiar in some later twentieth-century music, it is remarkable how fresh still are the challenges of such music as this. Pierrot is contemplating the horror of death here, and we cannot expect Schoenberg to animate it in a C major waltz. Again it is worth taking note of Anthony Payne's insight into the type of composition we are dealing with:

One type of movement . . . arguably the most obvious outcome of Expressionism's subconscious delving, is exemplified in the last of the Five Orchestral Pieces, the third of the Three Piano Pieces Opus 11, and 'Enthauptung' from *Pierrot*. Here one finds the freely associative connexions of subconscious logic fully in play . . . part of the expressive idea would seem to be to provide a symbol of something impossible to perceive direct. Such is the speed and density of Schoenberg's feeling in time, and so far beyond simple understanding are the complex patterns of subconscious experience he is attempting to shape in his art, that a symbol is required which we can never really recall in detail. Experience almost too bewildering for the human mind to encompass is given an appropriate representation.[25]

The bass clarinet, viola and cello are joined by the flute in a fourteen-and-a-half bar transition, the last *Pierrot* music to be composed. Brinkmann shows how in one three-bar sketch for a transition Schoenberg brought together no less than twelve motivic ideas from seven different numbers, so that 'not a single note in this montage, this motif-puzzle, is freely composed.'[26] Nor is the eventual transition 'freely composed', for it is based on 'Der kranke Mond', with a shortened version of the flute part;

the other instruments paraphrase some of the vocal material, beginning canonically, then provide homophonic accompaniment, a clarinet solo finally repeating the *Sprechstimme* cadence phrase mentioned under No. 7. Apart from being of great beauty, this transition is cleverly multifunctional. Obviously, it has a formal function in recapitulating the end of Part I for the closing phases of Part II, and it is tempting to feel that it to some extent compensates for the textural vacuum of 'Der kranke Mond'. It also separates the piano-soaked sound of 'Enthauptung' from the rugged piano solo that is to follow. Further, a narrative function is in play. Rather as in 'Der kranke Mond', where we leave behind Pierrot and the sombre moon, so the text of 'Enthauptung' marks the end of the florid Pierrot and the fearsome moon – a parallelism that the transitional paraphrase underlines wordlessly in its reference to the end of Part I.

(. . . carry straight on)

14 Die Kreuze   The Crosses

[piano, later with flute, clarinet in A, violin, cello: slow]

Heilge Kreuze sind die Verse,	Holy crosses are the verses
Dran die Dichter stumm verbluten,	whereon poets bleed in silence,
Blindgeschlagen von der Geier	blinded by a flock of vultures
Flatterndem Gespensterschwarme!	fluttering round in spectral swarms.
In den Leibern schwelgten Schwerter,	In their bodies swords have feasted,
Prunkend in des Blutes Scharlach!	glorying in their robes of scarlet!
Heilge Kreuze sind die Verse,	Holy crosses are the verses
Dran die Dichter stumm verbluten.	whereon poets bleed in silence.
Tot das Haupt – erstarrt die Locken -	Dead, the head - matted the tresses –
Fern, verweht der Lärm des Pöbels.	far and faint the noisy people.
Langsam sinkt die Sonne nieder,	Slowly sinks the sun in splendour,
Eine rote Königskrone. –	like a crimson kingly crown.
Heilge Kreuze sind die Verse!	Holy crosses are the verses.

The first verse figures a harsh piano solo. Then flute, clarinet, and violin and cello (on harmonics) enter for a quiescent portrayal of 'death', after which the tutti builds to a climax on bar 17 with trills in all instruments (tremolando in the piano) as the last line of Part II is intoned. In isolation, there are features here to put off the most ardent devotee: the crashing complexity of the piano, the cacophonous climax, the wearing emphasis in most of the bars on the principal rhythm in various 'clever' rhythmic augmentations and diminutions, the utterly unsophisticated repetition of the opening two chords as the last two. The 'extreme emotionality' of this setting[27] was, though, fully thought out, for 'Die Kreuze' was completed on 9 July 1912 when all the other twenty melodramas had been finalized. Its justification is both local and strategic. The intensity of the 'Enthauptung' before it is earnest. It would be hard to find a light, ironical or satirical tone in that text, and the music would not betray it even if there were one. The task of 'Die Kreuze' is not to match or even transcend that intensity but take the threat of reality away – to trump tragedy with fantasy.

If we feel there is sanctimony in No. 14 to the point of being laughable, when for the third time we have it shrieked at us that 'Holy crosses are the verses' while the little chamber group makes a pathetic attempt at a Wagnerian climax, then Schoenberg has succeeded. And this is a strategic apex of *Pierrot*, for Part III is to be refined, nostalgic, artfully wicked: only the most pungent characterizations in Part II can hope to live through to the end in our residual, overall impression of the work.

PART III

15 Heimweh | Nostalgia

[clarinet in A, violin, piano, later with piccolo and cello: flexible tempo]

Lieblich klagend – ein kristallnes Seufzen	Sweet lamenting, like a crystal sighing,
Aus Italiens alter Pantomime,	rises from the old Italian comedy,
Klingts herüber: wie Pierrot so hölzern,	sadly asking: why's Pierrot so wooden,
So modern sentimental geworden.	in the sentimental modern manner?
Und es tönt durch seines Herzens Wüste,	And it echoes through his heart's desert
Tönt gedämpft durch alle Sinne wieder,	echoes mutedly through all his senses –
Lieblich klagend – ein kristallnes Seufzen	sweet lamenting, like a crystal sighing
Aus Italiens alter Pantomime.	rising from the old Italian comedy.
Da vergisst Pierrot die Trauermienen!	Then Pierrot forgets his tragic manner!
Durch den bleichen Feuerschein des Mondes,	Through the silver fiery glow of moonlight,
Durch des Lichtmeers Fluten – schweift die Sehnsucht	through a flood of radiance swells his yearning,
Kühn hinauf, empor zum Heimathimmel,	boldly soars on high to skies of homeland –
Lieblich klagend – ein krystallnes Seufzen!	sweet lamenting like a crystal sighing.

59

Part III has been understood as the most coherent section from the point of view of textual themes. These are explicit in 'Heimweh', where Pierrot is nostalgic about his home (see No. 20) and about the old Italian comedy which is, broadly, the topic of Nos. 16–19. Perhaps the most indicative line is at the beginning of the third verse.

It may be because of the absence of any systematic compositional process that the music of 'Heimweh' has been little discussed. Yet in sophistication of contrast and elaboration it surpasses anything to be found elsewhere in *Pierrot*. An opening piano figure captures the 'crystal' sigh to be mentioned three times in the text. Then the first part of the body of the melodrama is dominated by a lyrical violin line (bars 1–12) that is one of the most sustained melodies in *Pierrot*. The end of the second verse sets the repeated opening two lines in quite a new light, with pulsating puppet music in which the violin's quaver groupings of double stops against a Jewish-sounding clarinet cannot fail to remind us of what was to come in Stravinsky (in particular *The Soldier's Tale*, 1918). The violin again dominates the following passage of arpeggio flourishes (clarinet) as well as trills (piano) leading to a subtly undramatic peak at the word 'Trauermienen'. The challenge for Schoenberg here was to portray not a tragic manner, but a tragic manner that is forgotten: thus the climax is not dwelt on, and gives way in bar 20 to subdued 'Mondestrunken' material (and a referential piano chord which has been emphasized in bars 1–4, and 11). But this in turn proves to be the beginning of a denouement which reveals the very essence of nostalgia, of hot reality cancelled by the bleak sighs of bars 25–6 (see Ex. 14).

However superficially, at least this description acknowledges the richness of a musical scene of some six dramatic elements. And there is yet more, for a four-bar transition follows in which a jagged, 'mock' virtuosic cello solo (with piano, clarinet and piccolo) breaks the mood to prepare for the following pantomime.

(. . . no pause)

16 Gemeinheit	Mean Trick!

[piccolo, clarinet in A, violin, cello, piano: fairly fast]

In den blanken Kopf Cassanders,	In the gleaming skull of Cassander,
Dessen Schrein die Luft durchzetert,	as he shrieks and cries blue murder,
Bohrt Pierrot mit Heuchlermienen,	bores Pierrot with hypocritic kindness –
Zärtlich – einen Schädelbohrer!	and a cranium-borer.

Ex. 14: 'Heimweh', bars 20–7

Darauf stopft er mit dem Daumen	And then presses with his finger
Seinen echten türkschen Taback	very genuine Turkish tobacco
In den blanken Kopf Cassanders,	in the gleaming skull of Cassander,
Dessen Schrein die Luft durchzetert!	As he shrieks and cries blue murder!
Dann dreht er ein Rorh von Weichsel	Then screwing a cherry pipestem
Hinten in die glatte Glatze	firmly in the polished surface,
Und behäbig schmaucht und pafft er	at his ease he puffs away,
Seinen echten türkschen Taback	puffs on his genuine Turkish tobacco
Aus dem blanken Kopf Cassanders!	in the gleaming skull of Cassander!

'Gemeinheit' is a conspicuous text. Whereas some of the previous numbers have included one or two actions, moments of surprise or nasty revelations, few offer any routine sequence of events, yet No. 16 tells a simple, gruesome story with nonchalant linguistic clarity.

However gruesome, it is also delightfully playful. There is surely overt musical satire in the treatment of the lurching anacruses, at the end of bar 7, for example, in piccolo and clarinet, and in bar 19 where the composer instructs: 'broad upbeat'. This is a musical gesture very similar to those found in the first movement of Berg's violin concerto (1935), where Schoenberg's pupil wrote 'Wienerisch' (Viennese) on the score, partly so that conductor and players would know the style of rubato needed – a style that cannot easily be described verbally. In the spirit of playfulness, the *Sprechstimme* is delivered haltingly with many short rests making us wait for the next humorous word or clause. The word 'zärtlich', for example, decorated with a mordent to suggest a little ironic crack in the voice, is followed by a coquettish silence (beginning of bar 7) and then the 'dry' (in effect, spoken) announcement of the cranium-borer. The penultimate example of this halting effect, in bars 23–4, records an inflection in German which is not captured by Porter's translation: after the two insertions of lines 1 and 7 'in[to]' Cassander's head, we find Pierrot at the end smoking – 'out' of it.

If the stages of the story are articulated by tempo, instrumentation and dynamics, nevertheless there is no development of the kind described in 'Heimweh'. On the contrary, Schoenberg produces a continual invention on the principal rhythm. However, his control of ongoing effect is once again in evidence. No other melodrama is so insistent on the principal rhythm, prominently and emphatically though it appears before and after. Yet in 'Gemeinheit' a deft change in the accentuation (from ♪ ♪ ♪ | ♪ ♪ ♪ ♪ elsewhere to ♪ ♪ ♪ | ♪ ♪ ♪ ♪ here) once again guarantees a balance of contrast with unity that is at least akin to what we would expect of a continuous dramatic composition.

(. . . long, attenuated pause)

17 Parodie	Parody

[piccolo, clarinet in A, viola, piano]

Stricknadeln, blank und blinkend,	Knitting needles, brightly twinkling,
In ihrem grauen Haar,	stuck in her graying hair,
Sitz die Duenna murmelnd,	sits the Duenna mumbling,
Im roten Röckchen da.	wearing her short red dress.
Sie wartet in der Laube,	She's waiting in the arbor,
Sie liebt Pierrot mit Schmerzen,	she loves Pierrot with anguish.
Stricknadeln, blank und blinkend,	Knitting needles, brightly twinkling,
In ihrem grauen Haar.	stuck in her graying hair.
Da plötzlich – horch! - ein Wispern!	But sudden - hark – a whisper!
Ein Windhauch kichert leise:	a wind-puff titters softly:
Der Mond, der böse Spötter,	the moon, that cruel mocker,
Äfft nach mit seinen Strahlen –	is mimicking with moonbeams
Stricknadeln, blink und blank.	knitting needles twinkling bright.

In general, *Pierrot* comes over nicely in translation, and it would be precious to insist that only a performance in German is a 'true' rendering. Nevertheless, 'Parodie' is an illustration of what may be lost in translation. 'Stricknadeln, blink und blank' is a kind of sound poetry that cannot be captured in English. Even at the tiniest level of phonemic resonance all is lost – for 'Strick-' in line 1 carries the momentary and in this context entirely plausible meaning, 'rope-', whereas '[k]nit-' in English cannot do the same linguistic work. Grammatically too there are some insurmountable translation problems in *Pierrot* of which the last line of 'Parodie' is an extreme case. Neither the good solution of turning 'brightly twinkling' into 'twinkling bright', nor others that have been tried, can match Hartleben's original twist at 'blink und blank'. For all that, the imagery of 'Parodie' is scintillating in any language, and its placing is inspired. It shows Pierrot as passive between the lurid activity in 'Gemeinheit' and anxiety of 'Der Mondfleck', yet keeps him 'on stage' for this suite of six named appearances (see above, p. 51). It reintroduces a female character, absent since No. 12, and in the third verse the moon too reappears.

Much attention has been given in the past to those aspects of 'Parodie' and No. 18, 'Der Mondfleck', which are most apparent musically – their contrapuntal devices. In 'Parodie' there are three canonic species. First, viola and voice proceed by canon at the unison with clarinet intervening in inverted canon at the ninth. A different species takes over from bar 16, where voice and piccolo begin in canon at the unison, and viola and clarinet use different material in inverted canon at the tritone. Later (bar 22) voice and clarinet are paired against flute and viola in yet a different species. It will be noted that the 'voice', for all the strict compositional relationships to be read from the score, is nevertheless still *Sprechstimme*, with no special instruction to convey the pitches. The interaction of calculation and coincidence is further reflected in the relationship between all these combinations and the piano, which accompanies rhapsodically, occasionally picking up cues from the other instruments, but mostly not (once again referential material is obvious – compare the opening, right hand, with bars 16, left hand, 17, right hand, and 27, left hand).

Any writer may be forgiven for not knowing what to make of the appearance of such compositional strictness in an opus of such apparent freedom. Austin, for example, doubts if it is 'at all possible or desirable' to hear the harmonic relation of the individual parts; 'And if the harmony is negligible, then the canons do not make polyphony in the traditional sense of this word, but rather a loosely woven texture that needs a new name.'[28] This issue will be taken up in discussion of the next melodrama. Meanwhile, however, the reader might contemplate what could be more apt in a melodrama entitled 'Parody', featuring knitting-needles, than a texture of contrapuntally related lines, perceptibly 'woven' as Austin states.

A stormy two-bar piano transition introduces not only the serious mood of 'Der Mondfleck', but also its rhythmic motives and melodic shapes. In light of the extraordinary compositional structure that is to unfold, and the learned exposition of its compositional elements pounded out here on the piano, the transition may be intended as, or at least the opportunity for, a musicians' joke – Schoenberg announcing that the following item is not best described as freely improvised.

(. . . no pause)

18 Der Mondfleck	The Moonfleck

[piccolo, clarinet in B♭, violin, cello, piano: very fast]

Einen weissen Fleck des hellen Mondes	With a snowy fleck of shining moonlight
Auf dem Rücken seines schwarzen Rockes,	on the back side of his smart new frockcoat,

So spaziert Pierrot im lauen Abend,	so sets forth Pierrot one balmy evening,
Aufzusuchen Glück und Abenteuer.	in pursuit of fortune and adventure.
Plötzlich stört ihn was an seinem Anzug,	Sudden - something's wrong with his appearance,
Er beschaut sich rings und findet richtig –	he looks round and round and then he finds it –
Einen weissen Fleck des hellen Mondes	there's a snowy fleck of shining moonlight
Auf dem Rücken seines schwarzen Rockes.	on the back side of his smart new frockcoat.
Warte! denkt er: das ist so ein Gipsfleck!	Hang it! thinks he: a speckle of plaster!
Wischt und wischt, doch – bringt ihn nicht herunter!	Wipes and wipes, but he can't make it vanish!
Und so geht er, giftgeschwollen weiter,	On he goes, his pleasure has been poisoned,
Reibt und reibt bis an den frühen Morgen –	rubs and rubs until it's almost morning
Einen weissen Fleck des hellen Mondes.	at a snowy fleck of shining moonlight.

'Mondfleck' is a *tour de force* in many respects, not the least of which may be the number of words that have been written about it. As often happens in musical historiography, these have included a misconception carried from one commentary to the next, originating in Wellesz's description 'a double canon *cancrizans*, between piccolo and clarinet on the one hand, and violin and cello on the other.'[29] Schoenberg corrected this in his own copy of Wellesz, so we now have the composer's own analysis: 'fugue between piccolo and clarinet on the one hand, canon between violin and cello on the other.'[30] This is not the complete picture, for the outer voices of the piano are in augmented canon with piccolo and clarinet (lower and upper voices respectively – that is, in inverted counterpoint). Further, and most famously, the second half of the melodrama is, in the pitches and rhythms of both woodwind and strings, designed as a strict retrograde of the first half, from the middle of bar 10. Retrogrades were to become central in the compositional techniques of Schoenberg's star pupils: not only in the twelve-note methods of Webern, but also in Berg, in whose structural designs large-scale retrogrades are so important a feature that, 'with the exception of the Violin Concerto, there is not a single major work [after Op.

5] that does not include one.'[31] 'Design' and execution are a touch out of kilter in 'Der Mondfleck', for Schoenberg made four tiny errors in transcribing the retrograde, one of rhythm that he corrected in his own printed score, and three of pitch.[32] He may never have noticed the 'wrong' notes. Yet there are minor errors, in 'strict' twelve-note works, that on being challenged he refused to correct subsequently, on the grounds that composerly intuition must override all retrospective laws of composition.

It is quite possible to conclude that all Schoenberg achieves with his contrapuntal cunning in No. 18 is a 'loosely woven texture' (see p. 65 above), especially if it is felt that 'Der Mondfleck' has been, and is continually likely to be, over-admired as 'one of the most elaborate canons worked out since the end of the fifteenth century.'[33] The range of critical response is compounded when not only are the musical results questioned, but the informed view is also added that, in any case, complex imitative writing is no great achievement if the harmony is fully 'free' (this latter point will remind the reader of what was said about 'Enthauptung'). However, there are two distinct aspects of this music. On the one hand, the elaboration of a vivid instrumental texture through partly perceptible contrapuntal devices is a traditional, respectable way to compose. Not only that, but in an 'atonal' music, with a succession of short and distinct musical ideas, in instrumentation that yields exceptional sonic clarity, what is effective forwards is more than likely to be effective backwards. On the other hand, 'Der Mondfleck' is simply not a retrograde structure as a whole, since recitation and pianist, the joint backbone of *Pierrot*, are through composed just as the text is continuous.

One way or another, any unidimensional view of No. 18 is certain to mislead, so compelling is the internal musical evidence that Schoenberg was responding procedurally to the inherent duality of the poem. It has been noted often that the point of musical retrogression represents Pierrot looking around, and that the 'fleck' remains ineradicable until night, the canon, has run its course. This is an example of criticism sensitive to the ambiguity of the number as a whole, even if we might think 'perhaps so, perhaps not'. We might care to take the literalist view that the composer is unlikely to portray, in a concrete musical way, something that is symbolic rather than actual, for Pierrot cannot literally turn around to see his own back. And we might thus be missing the artistically obvious: one of Schoenberg's most memorable oil paintings – he was much preoccupied with visual art at this period (see various comments in chapter 2) – is of himself walking into the middle distance, 'Self-portrait from behind'.[34]

Selbstporträt von hinten is dated April 1911, just over a year before 'Der Mondfleck'.

(. . . no long pause)

19 Serenade   Serenade

[cello, piano, later with flute, clarinet in A, violin: very slow waltz]

Mit groteskem Riesenbogen	With a bow grotesquely monstrous
Kratzt Pierrot auf seiner Bratsche,	scrapes Pierrot on his viola.
Wie der Storch auf einem Beine,	Like a stork on one leg standing
Knipst er trüb ein Pizzicato.	sadly plucks a pizzicato.
Plötzlich naht Cassander – wütend	Sudden! here's Cassander,
Ob des nächtgen Virtuosen –	raging at the night-time virtuoso.
Mit groteskem Riesenbogen	With a bow grotesquely monstrous
Kratzt Pierrot auf seiner Bratsche.	scrapes Pierrot on his viola.
Von sich wirft er jetzt die Bratsche:	Then he throws aside viola:
Mit der delikaten Linken	with a delicate use of the left hand
Fasst den Kahlkopf er am Kragen –	seizes Cassander by the collar –
Traümend spielt er auf der Glatze	dreaming plays upon his bald head
Mit groteskem Riesenbogen.	with a bow grotesquely monstrous.

Although the clowning is not yet over, the heights of musical excitement are, for this last phase of Op. 21 is to calm *Pierrot* to a peaceful close with a serenade, a barcarolle, and the quiet closing song 'O alter Duft'. 'Heimfahrt' followed 'Serenade' in Schoenberg's manuscript from the earliest written conception, so that the transition which links them was not an afterthought (bars 46–53, where flute, clarinet and violin join the cello and piano). His work on 'O alter Duft' began after this, and it too is preceded by a short transition with a foretaste of its main melodic motive. In other words, Nos. 19–21 form a triptych, deliberately, carefully, flowing through to the final silence.

Picking up the thread of 'Colombine' and 'Valse de Chopin', 'Serenade' is a waltz 'to be performed very freely' by cellist and pianist. The instrumental introduction is the longest in *Pierrot*, and the only one to have the effect of a prolonged and relatively self-contained musical section. Even this new turn of events, however, can be regarded as the outcome of a process, at least in the sense that the cello has been increasingly prominent in Part III, in the transition between Nos. 15 and 16, and in No. 16 itself. It was thus the most recently featured solo instrument, for in Nos. 17 and 18, the piano transition aside, there is a constant battery of instruments.

Schoenberg quotes from this music in the essay 'Brahms the Progressive':

Illustrations of the tendency toward asymmetrical construction among post-Wagnerian composers are very numerous. Though the natural inclination to build two- and four-measure phrases is still present, deviation from multiples of two is achieved in many fashions . . . The 'cello solo from 'Serenade' . . . consists of an irregular change of one- and two-measure units.

. . . deviations from simple construction . . . have become incorporated into the syntax and grammar of perhaps all subsequent musical structures. Accordingly, they have ceased to be recorded as merits of a composition – though unfortunately many illiterate composers still write two plus two, four plus four, eight plus eight unchangingly.[35]

Some of the text/music relationship in 'Serenade' has been discussed already in chapter 3 (see pp. 24–5 above). It remains to be noted the flexibility with which Schoenberg moves through the narrative – for again this number is a 'story' in the manner of 'Gemeinheit'. The sweeping cello lines lead to a cadenza preceding the second verse, then 'brilliant' semiquavers in the principal rhythm at Cassander's entry, followed by a slow melody, over a piano ostinato, reaching high D (two octaves above middle C), and a high 'flowing' passage to represent the dreamy bowing on a bald head.

(. . . go on directly, with no pause)

20 Heimfahrt (Barcarole)   Journey Homeward (Barcarolle)
[flute, clarinet in A, violin, cello, piano: gently animated]

Der Mondstrahl ist das Ruder,	A moonbeam is the rudder,
Seerose dient als Boot:	waterlily serves as boat,
Drauf fährt Pierrot gen Süden	and so Pierrot goes southward
Mit gutem Reisewind.	with friendly following wind.
Der Strom summt tiefe Skalen	The stream hums scales beneath him
Und wiegt den leichten Kahn.	and rocks the fragile craft.
Der Mondstrahl ist das Ruder,	A moonbeam is the rudder,
Seerose dient als Boot.	waterlily serves as boat.
Nach Bergamo, zur Heimat,	To Bergamo, his homeland,
Kehrt nun Pierrot zurück,	at last Pierrot returns;
Schwach dämmert schon im Osten	soft glimmers rise to eastward,
Der grüne Horizont.	the green of the horizon.
- Der Mondstrahl ist das Ruder.	A moonbeam is the rudder.

The flute links Nos. 19 and 20, but the motion of the new music is set off by a rising and falling seven-pitch ostinato for pizzicato cello and violin (with mutes). Its harmonic effect is similar to that of the piano ostinato which initiates *Pierrot*, and with which it has four common pitches; the first three notes are the same as those of the piano in bar 1 of 'Serenade'. The clarinet too, in the solo part from bar 3, is familiar, using a rhythmic motive that recalls, for one example of many possible, the 'schwungvoll' tune in 'Valse de Chopin' quoted above (see example 6). In many other features we can hear 'Heimfahrt' as pulling together melodic, rhythmic and textural fragments from elsewhere. This is not a matter of goal direction – after all, at least eight other melodramas had yet to be completed when 'Heimfahrt' was finished. But one may suppose that in setting Pierrot's farewell Schoenberg gave free rein to the interplay of all the musical material on his desk.

It is 'woven' into an uninterrupted rocking motion exquisitely held back, rather as a single large wave can restrain the periodic rocking of a boat, by ritenutos at the first line of the poem and its central repetition (bars 14–5). Within this cameo Schoenberg takes up many suggestions from the fertile poetic stock of 'Heimfahrt'. Piano staccatos in bar 3 are marked 'like drops'. The 'moonbeam' in bar 6 is a soft, rapid flute ascent, and the flute describes the wind in bar 11 with a fluttertongue arpeggio. The deep 'scales' hummed by the wind are chromatic clusters in cello, violin and clarinet (bar 13). The 'glimmers' on the green horizon are delicate repeated notes in flute, clarinet, cello pizzicato and piano, and the rocking subsides with a fragmentary reference to the opening ostinato and clarinet motive (bars 26–7). For not a word of this account is there proof. Such are the effects, all the same, and Schoenberg was careful (in 1949) to note the importance of 'expression' of this kind:

In the preface to *Pierrot lunaire* I had demanded that performers ought not to add illustrations and moods of their own derived from the text. In the epoch after the First World War, it was customary for composers to surpass me radically, even if they did not like my music. Thus when I had asked not to add external expression and illustration they understood that expression and illustration were out, and that there should be no relation whatsoever to the text . . . What nonsense! What is the purpose of adding music to a text? . . . Besides, how do you make sure that your music does not express something – or more: that it does not express something provoked by the text?[36]

As the Barcarolle fades out we are left with a three-note descent for cello and clarinet in thirds (bars 29–30), and a mild punctuating piano chord (reading upwards from the bass: B, A, E, G, readily heard as a dominant chord of the E tonality outlined at the beginning of No. 21). This is a favourite moment to those who know *Pierrot*, since it announces melodically and harmonically the opening material of the last, most beautiful melodrama.

(. . . no pause!)

21 O alter Duft	O Ancient Scent

[flute (piccolo), clarinet in A (bass clarinet in B♭), violin (viola), cello, piano: with movement]

O alter Duft aus Märchenzeit	O ancient scent from fabled times,
Berauschest wieder meine Sinne!	once more you captivate my senses!
Ein närrisch Heer von Schelmerein	A merry troupe of roguish pranks
Durchschwirrt die leichte Luft.	pervades the gentle air.
Ein glückhaft Wünschen macht mich froh	With cheerful longing I return
Nach Freuden, die ich lang verachtet:	to pleasure I too long neglected.
O alter Duft aus Märchenzeit	O ancient scent from fabled times,
Berauschest wieder mich!	once more you captivate me.
All meinen Unmut gab ich preis,	All of my gloom I've set aside:

Aus meinen sonnumrahmten Fenster	and from my sun-encircled window
Beschau ich frei die liebe Welt	I gladly view the lovely world,
Und träum hinaus in selge Weiten . . .	and dreams go forth to greet the distance . . .
O alter Duft – aus Märchenzeit!	O ancient scent from fabled times!

The very last valediction was in reality the last text Schoenberg decided to include in *Pierrot* and the last new composition to be started (though 'Gemeinheit' and 'Die Kreuze' had not been completed). There is a strong kinship between the opening of 'O alter Duft' and the famous soprano entry in the finale of Schoenberg's Second String Quartet, Op. 10 (1908), 'Ich fühle Luft von anderem Planeten' (I feel the air from another planet): they share a transcendental stillness, and bitter-sweet quasi-tonality. Historians have been quick to observe that it is 'tonality' which Schoenberg intended to be associated with the idea of a 'scent' regained, a tonality hinted at by repeated focus on the E major triad (as well as D major in bar 6), and an E octave in the bass at the end (bar 29).

Yet we should beware of too grandiose an interpretation. For one thing, 'O alter Duft' did not strike all contemporaries as being notable for its return to tonality: Wellesz, for instance, merely noted that this 'dreamy, tender, and thoroughly simple song, has the effect of a free improvisation.'[37] Moreover, we must not discount the nostalgic exposure here of overt contrapuntal devices which Stuckenschmidt found striking – 'the simple main theme appears diminished, inverted, in three-part chords, varied in figuration and in a canon between its own diminution and its inversion'[38]; nor must the larger historical perspective make us lose sight of the fact that the main theme presents, both in crotchets and quavers, the principal rhythm. And 'O alter Duft' is the only item to use all eight instruments, but with the opening and closing notes for piano alone, and solo *Sprechstimme* in the final bar.

All of this points directly to the 'fabled times' that have unrolled in *Pierrot* itself, in a spirit of reconciliation, even consolation, but with the promise of continuing revival of the fantasy world in a last, alienating word, 'Märchenzeit'.

5

A brief afterword

If there is a consensus about the writing of history, it is that what is more recent in the 'known' world is more difficult to command. In answer to the question 'what has been the importance of *Pierrot* since 1912?', it may well be that the wisest response is to claim that it is far too early to say. Certainly Schoenberg's own attempts, not only to write contemporaneous history, but also to predict the future of 'classical' music, can now be seen as partly flawed, and some would say fundamentally misconceived.

During his lifetime, Schoenberg witnessed a continual cultural struggle between modernism and traditionalism. In this arena, though he was revered by some of those artists for whom he had the most respect, he could not hope to be popular musically in the sense that the composers of his youth had been. His claim to have found inspiration in the 'great' composers of the past, above all in Mozart, probably did more harm than good. His followers could see the purely musical points he was making, but among the music-loving public, which would much prefer to listen to Mozart's music than to Schoenberg's, the very idea of Mozart being held responsible for this distant musical descendant could only be a genealogical nightmare. Schoenberg's argument in the famous essay 'Brahms the Progressive' that Brahms was a more advanced composer than Wagner could make sense only at a highly technical level, and could not but mystify the average listener to 'Brahms 3' in the concert hall one day, and Wagner's *Tristan* in the opera house the next. His championing of the music of his immediate hero, Gustav Mahler, which was virtually unknown outside Vienna, added to the peculiarity of the Schoenbergian view of music history. Meanwhile, the Romantic 'great man' theory of music history[1] was being nourished by the increasing public worship of Debussy, whose professional status as the father of modern music did nothing to diminish the public enjoyment of his more accessible scores, and of Stravinsky, who throughout Schoenberg's period of dodecaphonic composition between the world wars offered one new delicious 'neo-classical' work after another. In general, perhaps

Schoenberg would have done better to keep quiet and let his music speak for itself; but that was not his way.

It was perhaps only after Schoenberg's death in 1951 that the seeds he had sown flowered in unexpected ways. It turned out that his brilliant pupil Webern had provided the path to the new music that captured European and American imagination in the 1950s, a path that converged with another apparent mainstream stemming from Debussy, through Messiaen to Pierre Boulez (born 1925). Had Schoenberg lived to see the impact of Webern's music, he would surely have been astonished and uncomprehending. It turned out that 'experimental' composition was to become the norm and traditionalism would be backed against the wall. Had Schoenberg lived inordinately into the mid–1960s, to contemplate his imminent centenary in 1974, he might also have been shocked to see what happens when the 'new' becomes a real yardstick in societal terms, far beyond the remit of high culture. It turned out, further, that among interested composers Schoenberg's music, not because of *Pierrot*, but because of his later dodecaphonic 'classics', was in danger of coming to be seen as that of an old fogey.

However, at the same time the very idea of a 'mainstream' was being challenged from almost as many directions as one can think of, directions of which Schoenberg had not the least inkling. Society – affluent Western society – became a melting pot of what seems nowadays an extreme plurality. Is it micro-electronics that is really pushing music into it future? Is it 'popular' music – that is, will a future dictionary of music have an entry for '*Sergeant Pepper*' somewhere between 'Schoenberg' and '*Sprechstimme*'? Is 'tonality' to return, and make some of the musical twentieth century seem like an atonal hiccup? Can a return of 'tonality' resist the transcultural sweep of the modern, pantonal musical world in any case? All told, can a defenceless little piece like *Pierrot*, hatched on a determined whim decades ago, still performable only by experts, survive in a post-modern environment?

There is every reason to suppose that it can. It originated, rather quickly (but see pp. 25–6 above), in an outburst of only nine 'entirely atonal' completed works by Schoenberg (to follow Bryan Simms's count)[2] over roughly a decade. It took Europe by storm just before the First World War, fascinating composers not only of the Second Viennese tendency, but as outside that and as distinct as Puccini and Stravinsky; and attracting as much press attention as any of the Diaghilev ballets (such as the revolutionary *Rite of Spring*). Schoenberg toured *Pierrot* around Europe shortly after the First World War, and again it was profoundly influential, as much written about as if it were a new work, though it was some ten years old. He returned to it living in Los Angeles during the Second World War, when a recording was made (see p. 77 below), one of the many that continue to appear.

Pierrot took deep root in twentieth-century music. One of the subsequent masterpieces of the post-war period, Boulez's *Le Marteau sans màitre*, is fundamentally inspired by *Pierrot* – Boulez assesses the distance between these works in 'Speaking, Playing, Singing'.[3] Hundreds of other compositions have arisen in its elaborate wake, from Stravinsky's *The Soldier's Tale* through to the present-day tradition of music-theatre.

Perhaps even more important is the fact that *Pierrot* established chamber music as a genre independent of the ghost of Beethoven's string quartets. No-one, from Mendelssohn to Carter, Debussy and Schoenberg themselves included, ever really thought they could write a string quartet better than Beethoven did, only that they might do something different and worthwhile: many composers since 1912 have been convinced that they can write in the genre of *Pierrot*, approximately, and have tried, probably in the same spirit. The history of the influence of *Pierrot* in twentieth-century music is yet to be written, and may be better written in the early years of the next century when the many spin-offs will have found their historical destiny.

It would be an oversimplification to point to the genre enshrined in this work as its most conspicuous facet. It was its modernism and integrity that put it into the canon of great art. Not only has *Pierrot* seeped into many a pore of music in this century, but, given the storms it has weathered, there is no reason why it should not continue to exert influence in the next. As Boulez has said, 'it was at the exact moment when [Schoenberg] was most acutely aware of the transitory and its impact that he played a unique role as a composer.'[4] *Pierrot* won't go away, and there is nothing in post-modernism to suggest why it should.

75

Notes

1 The immortal Pierrot

1 These considerations are explored in detail in chapter 4.
2 *The Music of Stravinsky* (London, Routledge, 1988), p. 32
3 This conception is described by Willi Reich in *Schoenberg: A Critical Biography* (London, Longman, 1971), p. 74.
4 Quoted in *The Letters of Mozart and his Family*, ed. E. Anderson (London, Macmillan, 1966), pp. 630–1.
5 *Style and Idea: Selected Writings of Arnold Schoenberg*, ed. L. Stein, trans. L. Black (London, Faber, 1975), p. 145.
6 It is a revealing footnote on the historiography of the period that in the general literature on music 'melodrama' has been little studied as a genre, and it has generated relatively few pages of specialist research.
7 Hartleben's translation into German some three decades on of Albert Giraud's 'Pierrot' poems was an exceptionally free one.
8 *Der 'Blaue Reiter' Almanac*, ed. W. Kandinsky and F. Marc, trans. H. Falkenstein (New York, Viking, 1974; first published 1912), p. 147.
9 *The New Grove Dictionary*, vol. XII, p. 116.
10 M. Green and J. Swan, *The Triumph of Pierrot: The Commedia dell'Arte and the Modern Imagination* (New York, Macmillan, 1986), p.25
11 L. Jones, *Sad Clowns and Pale Pierrots* (Lexington, French Forum, 1984) p. 234.
12 S. Youens, 'The texts of *Pierrot lunaire*: an allegory of art and mind' in L. Stein (ed.), *From Pierrot to Marteau* (Los Angeles, Arnold Schoenberg Institute, 1987), p. 31.
13 Quoted in Reich, *Schoenberg*, p. 74.
14 *Orientations*, ed. J.-J. Nattiez (London, Faber, 1986), p. 342.
15 B. Simms, *Music of the Twentieth Century* (New York, Schirmer, 1986), p. 438.
16 *Music Since the First World War* (London, Dent, 1988), pp. 1–2.

2 Schoenberg, 1908–1912

1 *Schoenberg* (London, Dent, 1976), p. 7.
2 Quoted by Peyser in *The New Music: The Sense behind the Sound* (New York, Delta, 1971), p. 23.
3 Quoted by Smith in *Schoenberg and His Circle: A Viennese Portrait* (New York, Schirmer, 1986), p. 180.
4 *Mozart*, trans. M. Faber (New York, Vintage Books, 1982), p. 7.
5 *Style and Idea*, pp. 49–50.
6 *Style and Idea*, pp. 84–6.
7 *Style and Idea*, p. 88.
8 O. Neighbour, 'Schoenberg', in *The New Grove Second Viennese School*, ed. Stanley Sadie (London, Macmillan, 1983), p. 40.

9 *The Berg–Schoenberg Correspondence: Selected Letters*, eds. J. Brand, C. Hailey and D. Harris (London, Macmillan, 1987), p. 80.
10 *Style and Idea*, pp. 98–9.
11 It gives pause for thought that in the famous London Sinfonietta recording of Schoenberg's complete works for chamber ensemble, released for the 1974 centenary of the composer's birth, there is no f''' in *Herzgewächse*, but an e''', in tune with the instrumental e'' and e's that play against it – a point worth remembering for our subsequent considerations of pitch in *Pierrot*.
12 *Schoenberg* (Glasgow, Fontana, 1976), p. 47.
13 *Style and Idea*, pp. 50–1.

3 Genesis

1 In *Journal of the Arnold Schoenberg Institute*, 10/1 (1987), 11–27. Also of importance is his earlier, 1977 article 'On Pierrot's trail', *Journal of the Arnold Schoenberg Institute*, 2/1 (1977), 42–8.
2 E. Steuermann, *The Not Quite Innocent Bystander* (Lincoln, University of Nebraska, 1989), p. 35.
3 *Arnold Schoenberg* (London, Galliard, 1971; first published 1921), p. 139.
4 4th edn (London, Duckworth, 1974), p. 285.
5 G. Watkins, *Soundings: Music in the Twentieth Century* (New York, Schirmer, 1988), p. 185, my emphasis.
6 Performances of *Pierrot* using seven players with 'specialists' on bass clarinet and viola do occur. It is doubtful whether they can capture the integrated urgency of an 'authentic' performance.
7 *Schoenberg Remembered: Diaries and Recollections (1938–76)* (New York, Pendragon Press, 1980), pp. 186–7.
8 (Ann Arbor, UMI Research Press, 1979), p. 130.
9 See Brinkmann, 'On Pierrot's trail', 42–8.
10 E. Hilmar, *Arnold Schoenberg Gedenkausstellung 1974* (Vienna, Universal Edition, 1974), p. 235, No. 211.
11 H. Stuckenschmidt, *Arnold Schoenberg* (London, Calder, 1959), pp. 60–1.
12 *Style and Idea*, p. 55.
13 *Arnold Schoenberg*, pp. 7–8.

4 Pierrot lunaire

1 'Pitch class' is the current term for what the general reader might think of as a 'note name': pitch class C# means all notes called C# regardless of their octave disposition.
2 This term appears in Schoenberg's textbook *Fundamentals of Musical Composition* and elsewhere in his writings. It represents one of various fundamental features of tonal music which Schoenberg believed to be equally important in post-tonal composition.
3 *Soundings*, p. 185.
4 Further to the comments at the beginning of chapter 3, the reader may be willing to accept that this number is not fortuitous.
5 *Schoenberg*, p. 59.
6 *The Not Quite Innocent Bystander*, p. 172.
7 Perhaps the most frequently discussed case of *Klangfarbenmelodie* is the third of Schoenberg's Five Orchestral Pieces, Op. 16, which is in fact an elaborate quasi-canonic structure.
8 *Style and Idea*, pp. 281–2.
9 Schoenberg conveyed the tempo reduction very clearly when conducting the 1940 recording, nowadays available on CD (CBS MPK 45695).

10 This quotation, from previously unpublished papers, appeared in J. Dunsby and A. Whittall, *Music Analysis in Theory and Practice* (London, Faber, 1988), p. 76.
11 *Style and Idea*, pp. 81–2
12 A. Whittall, *Schoenberg Chamber Music* (London, BBC, 1972), p. 28.
13 *Style and Idea*, p. 146.
14 W. Austin, *Music in the Twentieth Century* (London, Dent, 1966), pp. 201–2.
15 Steuermann, *The Not Quite Innocent Bystander*, p. 37.
16 Kathryn Bailey comments on the shape of this melodrama in 'Formal organization and structural imagery in Schoenberg's *Pierrot lunaire*', *Studies in Music*, 2 (1977), 93–107.
17 *Schoenberg*, p. 60.
18 *Arnold Schoenberg*, p. 68.
19 *Schoenberg* (London, OUP, 1968), pp. 31–2.
20 *Arnold Schoenberg*, p. 67.
21 'What the sources tell us', 36.
22 *Schoenberg*, p. 64.
23 'Referential' is often applied to prominent recurrent pitches in 'atonal' music that seem to provide an overall aural focus. The analogy of the 'tonic' in tonal music is an informal indication of what is meant by 'referential'; but for the music theorist such analogy sidelines the very heart of understanding and explaining atonality itself.
24 F. Lesure, *Press-Book de Pierrot lunaire d'Arnold Schoenberg* (Geneva, Minkoff, 1985).
25 *Schoenberg*, p. 33.
26 'What the sources tell us', 22–3.
27 M. MacDonald, *Schoenberg*, p. 140.
28 *Music in the Twentieth Century*, pp. 209–10.
29 *Arnold Schoenberg*, p. 140.
30 R. Brinkmann, 'What the sources tell us', 26.
31 D. Jarman, *The Music of Alban Berg* (London, Faber, 1979), p. 185.
32 These are noted by Kathryn Bailey in 'Formal organization and structural imagery'.
33 C. Rosen, *Schoenberg*, p. 63.
34 This is reproduced in, among other sources, the MacDonald *Master Musicians* volume of 1976.
35 *Style and Idea*, pp. 424–8.
36 *Style and Idea*, pp. 145–6.
37 Wellesz, *Arnold Schoenberg*, p. 143.
38 Stuckenschmidt, *Arnold Schoenberg*, pp. 70–1.

5 A brief afterword

1 This is expounded in Allen's *Philosophies of Music History: a Study of General Histories of Music 1600–1900* (New York, Dover, 1962), p. 159.
2 *Music of the Twentieth Century*, p. 159.
3 *Orientations*, ed. J.-J. Nattiez (London, Faber, 1986), pp. 330–43.
4 *Orientations*, p. 329.

Select bibliography

The following is a list of works either to which a general reference is made above or, in most cases, from which actual quotations have been taken – a few of the quotations, of course, made only in order to be challenged, so that a listing may be anything but a recommendation. The list of works studied by the author in this project is very much longer, including the dissertation and article literature, of which some important items are in German; but where possible, I have specifically referred to, or quoted from, only material which is readily accessible in English, so that the reader can easily follow up my sources.

As a starting point for further reading, I recommend Oliver Neighbour's Schoenberg bibliography in *The New Grove Second Viennese School*, ed. S. Sadie (London, Macmillan, 1983), pp. 75–85. Extensive specialist bibliography, unfortunately now a few years out of date, is to be found in T. Satoh's *A Bibliographic Catalog . . .* (Tokyo, Kunitachi College, 1978), which was in its time an admirably comprehensive publication.

The attention of the non-academic reader is drawn to two bibliographic publications that may be consulted at good research libraries in universities or, say, capital cities: *The Music Index* is the music researcher's indispensable reference tool, more up to date and user-friendly than *Répertoire International de la Littérature Musicale*, which graduate students are routinely, and rightly, taught to consult; and the *Journal of the Arnold Schoenberg Institute* is a forum for research on the composer of *Pierrot* which tends to cull references to significant work surfacing through other publishing routes.

Abraham, G., *A Hundred Years of Music* (London, Duckworth, 4th edn., 1974)
Allen, W. D., *Philosophies of Music History: a Study of General Histories of Music 1600–1900* (New York, Dover, 1962)
Anderson, E., ed., *The Letters of Mozart and his Family* (London, Macmillan, 1966)
Austin, W., *Music in the Twentieth Century* (London, Dent, 1966)
Bailey, K. 'Formal organization and structural imagery in Schoenberg's *Pierrot*

lunaire', *Studies in Music*, 2 (1977), 93–107

Boulez, P., *Orientations*, ed. J.-J. Nattiez (London, Faber, 1986)

Brand, J., ed., *The Berg–Schoenberg Correspondence: Selected Letters*, with C. Hailey and D. Harris, eds. (London, Macmillan, 1987)

Brinkmann, R., 'On Pierrot's trail', *Journal of the Arnold Schoenberg Institute*, 2/1 (1977), 42–8

'What the sources tell us . . . a chapter of *Pierrot* philology', *Journal of the Arnold Schoenberg Institute*, 10/1 (1987), 11–27

Dunsby, J., '*Pierrot lunaire* and the resistance to theory', *The Musical Times*, 130 (1989), 732–6

Dunsby, J. and Whittall, A., *Music Analysis in Theory and Practice* (London, Faber, 1988)

Green, M. and Swan, J., *The Triumph of Pierrot: The Commedia dell'Arte and the Modern Imagination* (New York, Macmillan, 1986)

Hildesheimer, W., *Mozart*, trans. M. Faber (New York, Vintage Books, 1982)

Hilmar, E., *Arnold Schönberg Gedenkausstellung 1974* (Vienna, Universal Edition, 1974)

Jarman, D., *The Music of Alban Berg* (London, Faber, 1979)

Kandinsky, W., ed., *Der 'Blaue Reiter' Almanac*, with F. Marc, ed., trans. H. Falkenstein (New York, Viking, 1974; first published 1912)

Lessem, A., *Music and Text in the Works of Arnold Schoenberg: The Critical Years 1908–1922* (Ann Arbor, UMI Research Press, 1979)

Lesure, F., ed., *Press-Book de Pierrot lunaire d'Arnold Schönberg* (Geneva, Minkoff, 1985)

Macdonald, M., *Schoenberg* (London, Dent, 1976)

Maegaard, J., *Studien zur Entwicklung des dodekaphonen Satzes bei Arnold Schönberg* (Copenhagen, Wilhelm Hansen, 1972)

Meyer, L., *Emotion and Meaning in Music* (Chicago, University of Chicago, 1956)

Newlin, D., *Schoenberg Remembered: Diaries and Recollections (1938–76)* (New York, Pendragon Press, 1980)

Payne, A., *Schoenberg* (London, Oxford University Press, 1968)

Peyser, J., *The New Music: The Sense Behind the Sound* (New York, Delta, 1971)

Reich, W., *Schoenberg: A Critical Biography* (London, Longman, 1971)

Rognoni, L., *The Second Vienna School: Expressionism and Dodecaphony*, trans. R. Mann (London, Calder, 1977)

Rosen, C., *Schoenberg* (Glasgow, Fontana, 1976)

Rufer, J., *The Works of Arnold Schoenberg: a Catalogue of his Compositions, Writings and Paintings*, trans. D. Newlin (London, Faber, 1962)

Sadie, S., ed., *The New Grove Dictionary of Music and Musicians* (London, Macmillan, 1980)

Samson, J., *Music in Transition* (London, Dent, 1977)

Schoenberg, A., *Letters*, ed. L. Stein (London, Faber, 1964)

Style and Idea: Selected Writings of Arnold Schoenberg, ed. L. Stein, trans. L. Black (London, Faber, 1975)

Simms, B., *Music of the Twentieth Century* (New York, Schirmer, 1986)

Smith, J. A., *Schoenberg and his Circle: a Viennese Portrait* (New York, Schirmer, 1986)

Stein, L., ed., *From Pierrot to Marteau* (Los Angeles, Arnold Schoenberg Institute, 1987)

Steuermann, E., *The Not Quite Innocent Bystander* (Lincoln, University of Nebraska, 1989)

Stuckenschmidt, H., *Arnold Schoenberg* (London, Calder, 1959)

Walsh, S., *The Music of Stravinsky* (London, Routledge, 1988)

Watkins, G., *Soundings: Music in the Twentieth Century* (New York, Schirmer, 1988)

Wellesz, E., *Arnold Schoenberg* (London, Galliard, 1971; first published 1921)

Whittall, A., *Schoenberg Chamber Music* (London, BBC, 1972)

 Music Since the First World War (London, Dent, 1988)

Youens, S., 'The texts of *Pierrot lunaire*: an allegory of art and mind', in Stein (ed.), *From Pierrot to Marteau*, 30–2.

Index

(The following is an index to the main text and does not refer to prefatory material or the notes.)